The Care of Historical Collections

THE CARE
OF HISTORICAL
COLLECTIONS

A Conservation Handbook for the Nonspecialist

Per E. Guldbeck

American Association for State and Local History
Nashville: 1972

NOTE ON AUTHOR: Per Ernst Guldbeck is research associate with the
New York State Historical Association. He has degrees in anthropology
from the University of Denver and has done additional study at the
University of Hawaii and as a Scandinavian-American Foundation Fellow
to the University of Oslo. Prior to moving to Cooperstown, New York,
he had experience in the museum field as chief curator of the Museum of
International Folk Art in Santa Fe, New Mexico, and as archaeologist
at Mesa Verde National Park. In his present position he is primarily
responsible for exhibitions and the conservation of historic artifacts and
for teaching several courses related to this specialized field.

Dedicated to
Sheldon and Caroline Keck
Byberry Cottage

Foreword

A modern museum is an educational institution. While it shares certain philosophical and practical similarities with the other kinds of educational institutions—schools and libraries, for example—it is distinguished from others by one primary feature: it possesses collections of actual three-dimensional objects. Without objects, a museum cannot function in the ordinary sense; they are the central core around which it builds its program.

It follows that every museum has an imperative duty to take intelligent and effective care of the things in its possession, both while they are in storage and while they are on exhibition. Museums call this sort of care "conservation." A generation or two ago, there was very little specialized knowledge about the conservation of the objects in a typical historical collection. Common cleanliness, the prevention of rust, and similar ordinary housekeeping processes were about all that could be done, except perhaps for the most important specimens. A few major museums (often those which commanded elaborate laboratories and held highly significant items in their collections) were able to attack the problems of conservation with modern scientific and technological methods, and to work out more or less successful methods of treatment. Unfortunately these methods are sometimes quite complex and costly, and publications about them often presume considerable scientific knowledge and competence on the part of readers. There has continued to be a conspicuous lack of information about practical methods of day-to-day conservation for the less specialized history museum with modest technical and laboratory capacity. The same lack has been felt by private collectors who share the professional's concern for conservation.

It is this lack to which my long-time friend Per Guldbeck has addressed himself in this book. Without apologizing to the scientist for oversimplification, and without confusing the layman by too much complexity, he has provided a practical manual for those museum people who are seriously concerned—as all museum people should be—about the care of the objects in their custody. Per Guldbeck is not only a skilled conservator but an effective and popular teacher, who has worked and studied both in Europe and in the United States. Drawing on this broad experience, he has produced a book

vii

that will help all of us to ensure the continued survival of the objects which form our material inheritance from America's past.

H. J. SWINNEY

The Strong Museum
March, 1972

Preface

It was with some diffidence that this manual was undertaken, since there already exist excellent books on the conservation of historic materials. But as à result of speaking on the subject at a number of history museum meetings I began to realize that often there were more questions raised than answered.

Many of the people who have responsibility for the care of artifact collections come from small historical societies. They are uncertain as to how to proceed, what they can safely undertake, or where to buy the necessary equipment and supplies. In addition they are often overwhelmed by the technical literature and are not sure that they can understand it or translate it into practical use. Thus, this work has been prepared with the idea of providing small historical societies with an introduction to the problems of conservation and what can safely be done by the serious amateur.

Although this book was conceived primarily to aid the small historical society or museum—ranging in size from a one-man operation to a staff of five or six—it would be a mistake to assume that sheer numbers of staff guarantee that a collection will be cared for. Large institutions may put their energies into exhibition, education, or other activities at the expense of the basic collections which are the core of the institution's validity. The question then is not how large or small a staff you have, but how much time is devoted to the care of collections—and whether the people involved in the job have proper grounding in the philosophy of conservation and in the correct procedures.

This manual approaches the complex subject of conservation in three parts. The first consideration is for the health and safety of the total collection. What essential physical facilities will provide for the maximum life of a museum's collections. What requirements for storage and security are basic to the primary care of artifacts?

Regardless of how conducive the physical environment may be to the well-being of historic materials, sooner or later the museum staff will need to take more active and immediate measures to conserve a specific object. Section II considers two preliminaries to any conservation efforts. The nature and composition of the artifact must be identified and documented before the proper treatment can be determined; and the workshop area must provide a safe and controlled laboratory for that treatment. The final section of the manual discusses specific problems and methods in the conservation of artifacts and what first aid and repairs a nonspecialist dare undertake.

Bibliographies and supply lists are included at the end of each chapter. An introductory work like this does not pretend to cover the subject lest the general reader become overwhelmed by detail. Furthermore, other bibliographies, such as the New York State Historical Association's *Guide to Historic Preservation, Historical Agencies, and Museum Practices,* have been published for those concerned with delving more deeply into specific problem areas. The materials included here indicate sources the author personally has found helpful for guiding the director who has neither the time nor the staff to pursue a problem in depth. A work that attempts to précis the field of conservation encounters not only the possibility of errors, but of contrary opinions in approach to and methods of treating artifacts. For this reason I emphasize again that readers should and must make use of the reading lists and keep abreast of new literature.

Reading over the manuscript in galley proof, I was suddenly aware of how much of it was inadvertently a rephrasing of advice and lectures from many of my colleagues of the IIC and of how much I owe to them. Particular thanks for their inspiration and help over the years go to Dr. Robert Feller of the Mellon Institute, and Dr. Nathan Stolow of the National Gallery of Canada, whose fundamental scientific researches have contributed so much to the field of conservation.

I acknowledge real thanks to my friend and colleague, H. J. Swinney, director of the Margaret Woodbury Strong Museum, Rochester, New York, who edited this manuscript and recast it into clear language. I am also grateful to Harold Peterson of the U.S. National Park Service and to Mr. and Mrs. Sheldon Keck, noted conservators, who read and criticized various chapters. But any errors in fact or judgment are mine alone.

The philosophy of proper museum functions has changed over the years and will continue to change. At one time collecting and scholarship were considered most important. Then came the concept of expanded exhibitions, with popular lectures, traveling shows, school visits, and an increasing emphasis on interpretation and greater utilization of tactile senses. None of these approaches is in itself wrong. But so often in our attempt to win popularity with the public, the artifact becomes merely a pawn in the game, suffering attrition, damage, or loss. In considering the practice of conservation, remember that no matter what the present interpretative philosophy of your museum, the collection is its core. Only by proper concern for your artifacts will you be able to maintain your integrity as a professional.

Contents

xiii

xvi

THE HEALTH AND
SAFETY OF COLLECTIONS

PART

I

Conservation is an attempt to prolong the life of objects
of historical and artistic value. The primary job of
saving them can be done by their curators or owners
through providing proper safeguards for the objects
against environmental extremes: such as strong light,
humidity and temperature fluctuations; insects, animals,
and micro-organisms; vandalism or burglary
and curatorial ignorance or carelessness—the ravages
of man.

All of the above categories of conservation really
resolve themselves into one question: do you take care
of the artifacts you already have? Too often, in our
search for more or better pieces, we tend to neglect
an item we have already acquired. But if we do not
care for what we already own we have no moral
right to acquire more pieces. The principles of good
housekeeping—periodically checking items in the
storeroom and exhibit area for condition, and being
cautious about what objects go out on loan—may seem
mundane or tedious, but observation of these basic
principles can make even a small institution professional.

Conservation or restoration is sometimes likened to
the dramatic stories of surgeons saving people from
the consequences of disease or accident. Yet the
important part of conservation, like medicine, is
prevention rather than cure. An unskilled enthusiast
who undertakes to clean and repair an object often
lacks an understanding of materials and methods.
In his zeal he usually does too much rather than too
little, and sometimes does irreparable damage. It is

important never to do anything that you do not completely understand. Restraint and skill go hand-in-hand.

Because of the transitory nature of all materials, no one can completely stop their breakdown nor replace what is already gone. It is true that by a scientific study of the condition of an object and the nature of its materials, a skilled conservator may be able to prolong its life. He can also compensate for some losses. But he cannot wholly compensate for carelessness and ignorance on the part of those who have custody of the piece. Neither traditional techniques nor modern discoveries will extend the life of an object half as much as primary conservation—that is, proper care and maintenance of the objects in one's possession. We are only temporary custodians of antiquities, and it is our responsibility to see that they are passed on to the future.

1
Storage

Historical societies may have collections ranging in size from hatpins to manure wagons, and varying in fragility from delicate china figurines to cast iron cannon balls. Therefore flexible storage units that can be framed out of strong and adjustable materials are needed. "Dexion" or "Unistrut," two such materials, are structural steel channels in various lengths and gauges that can be bolted together. They can be disassembled for adjustment in size or for conversion to steps, worktables, or such other uses as may require a strong framework or support. If wooden framework is used, hardware stores and lumber yards can supply vertical metal stripping and spring clips or angle brackets which will allow shelving to be adjusted as desired. These shelves will not hold as heavy a load as steel channel, so exercise judgment.

Whichever structural material you use, you must eliminate the common storage problems of trying to squeeze an object into a tight space, or of piling a number of small objects one on another into a large boxy space. By these all-too-common practices, large objects are bent or broken, and small objects become inaccessible, with the wanted object invariably at the bottom of the pile. A crowded storage area results in frustration to the curator and damage to the objects. A clean, uncluttered, and well-organized storage area, plus periodic maintenance of it, may be more important to the long-range success of a historical society than an impressive exhibit in the main lounge with an inadequately-cared-for study collection to back it up.

A distinction must be made between storage of actual collection materials and storage of office supplies, periodicals, old correspondence, janitor's supplies, and exhibition supplies and props. Collections can be sorted in an infinite variety of ways depending on the size and nature of the individual objects. But keep in mind that a simplified classification of objects in storage and easy access to them are more practical than an elaborate finding and filing system which gets in the way or breaks down in use. This is particularly true if you are dealing with volunteer or part-time help who are not familiar with your system. It is a good idea to have maps or charts, both in your office and in the storage areas, to show the location of objects.

The storage area should have adequate and proper light (incandescent, to prevent fading of prints and textiles) and a few tables for examining or sorting objects. It should be as clean, well-ventilated, and humidity-controlled as your budget will allow. It should not suffer from neglect just because it is not in public view. This is especially important in old buildings where rats, mice, bats, squirrels, and insects can gain access. Dirty collections, and nutrient materials such as soap, wax, paper, glue, and excelsior strewn about will invite unwanted animal and insect visitors. A periodic check, plus a reliable pest-control service will help reduce the threat of animals and bugs. But just as important is the necessity of sealing and wrapping vulnerable materials and keeping the storage area clean—that dull but necessary chore of good housekeeping.

While a fireproof storage area is ideal, the hazards can still be minimized in old buildings by a few simple precautions. Do NOT smoke in a storage area. Do not store organic objects near heating pipes or radiators. Do not leave packing materials, cleaning rags, or oily cloths about. Remember also that objects such as old linens, woodenware, wax figurines, documents, and the like are highly flammable, especially in the dry storage conditions of many museums. Have fire extinguishers of the proper class near the doors and be sure they are inspected periodically.

Since water damage is almost as destructive as fire, ask yourself these questions. Are vulnerable objects stored under a leaky roof or eaves? Is storage far enough away from windows that if they are left open or broken, rain cannot harm the objects? Are overhead water, waste, or steam pipes tight and in good condition? If objects are in the basement, are the lowest shelves well above known flood levels? Is there a sump pump in the basement?

An additional note of caution for the safety of the person in charge of collections: there are any number of lethal artifacts in the average historical collection. Don't put heavy, rolling, or pointed objects at eye-level or overhead. Depending on the class of object, some shelves should be padded to minimize breakage, and some should have low rails or lips to keep objects from rolling or vibrating off.

Be careful about picking up broken glass, especially if it is from old medicine or chemical bottles. Watch out for splintery objects,

4

and keep up on your tetanus booster shots. Knives, saws, scissors, and other items from old medical kits may still contain living micro-organisms, and many of these kits still hold dandy "goodies" such as strychnine, opium, and morphine. Powder flasks and powder horns may contain black powder, just as potent today as the day it was made, and much more sensitive to friction than modern smokeless powders. There is a good chance that many of the muzzleloaders in your collection still have one or more live charges in them. Let an experienced person draw the charge, and don't fiddle with the hammer or trigger, lest you punch a hole through a colleague. An appalling number of so-called cannon balls (actually spherical shells) and grenades, from the Civil War period right up to the present, end up in historical societies, still live and fuzed. Do not on any account monkey with them! If you suspect that a shell is live, either dispose of it or call the nearest military base and ask someone with specific ordnance training in bomb disposal and defuzing to take over. The experts might suggest that some of your objects should be disposed of rather than defuzed. Even if it is your prized souvenir, take their word for it.

Storage of film may pose another safety hazard. If you have old nitrate-based movie film that is starting to acquire an oily feel, it should be disposed of. At this stage of chemical breakdown, film often becomes as sensitive and explosive as nitroglycerine. To determine whether your film has a nitrate base or the modern nonflammable acetate base, cut off an inch or so of film, grasp it in a pair of pliers, and light it with a match. If it is safety film it will curl and melt; but if it is nitrate base, it will burn instantly with no ash or residue. Check your films—you cannot afford to have such time bombs in your storage area.

SUGGESTED READING

Daifuku, H. "Collections, Their Care and Storage." In *The Organization of Museums: Practical Advice*, pp. 119-125. Paris: UNESCO, 1960.
Dunn, W. S., Jr. "Storing Your Collections: Problems and Solutions."

History News 25 (June 1970), Technical Leaflet #5, rev. ed.
Harvey, Virginia I. "Space and Textiles." *Museum News* 42 (November, 1963): 28-33.

SUPPLIES

Adjustable Metal for Shelves and Storage Racks
    Dexion, Inc. Woodside, N. Y.
    Unistrut Corporation, Wayne, Mich.

There are other metal-fabricating companies located around the country which make pre-fabricated shelving, storage cabinets, and lockers for storing collections. Consult the Yellow Pages of your area phone directory.

2
Security

In the interests of controlling your collections there should be limited access to the storage areas, and a limited number of keys. It is awkward to call the police and insurance company about a missing item only to find out later that it is hanging in the director's office, or a trustee has borrowed it, and that neither of them thought to notify you that they had removed it from storage.

Do you invite vandalism and/or burglary by the nature of your museum exhibits, your guards, or your personnel? How many unguarded exits do you have? Do you have unlocked windows, or easy access to a dark alley? Because one cannot easily change the location of an existing building, or for safety reasons lock certain doors during open hours, some of these questions may seem unfair. But the fact remains that collecting antiques is popular; prices are going up daily; and museums, having the bulk of antiques and paintings, are with few exceptions vulnerable to even a resolute 12-year-old with a pocket screwdriver. One cannot do much about the determined professional thief; one can, however, do something about tightening security to reduce the opportunity for theft.

Exhibits should be designed as far as possible without hidden corners which cannot be easily controlled by a guard; and vulnerable objects like early lighting devices, knives, firearms, jewelry, and primitive art should be well out of arm's reach or behind glass. So-called "psychological barriers" are as a rule effective only with the class of people who would not dream of touching or picking up objects anyway.

Buildings and grounds should be adequately lighted at night, especially hidden angles and rear entrances. There should be no close-up shrubbery for people to hide in, nor convenient painting ladders or construction scaffolds inviting second-story entrance. Keys to various buildings should be distributed only to people who actually need them, and a careful record of distribution should be kept. Often the number of keys a person has becomes a sort of status symbol, and in inverse proportion to his use for them. The more keys in circulation, the greater the chance for one to be lost. The upshot is the opportunity for unwarranted entry, or the expense of changing locks.

Guards are effective only in proportion to the care taken in selecting and training them. You should know something about their backgrounds and attitudes and should consider such questions as whether to have a guard deputized and bonded. Each guard should know the location of fire exits, hoses, electric switches and panels, manholes, water mains, and shutoffs, plus whatever special keys or wrenches are needed for access. In addition, the man on night watch should periodically check for unlocked windows and doors, leaking pipes, frozen radiators, missing items, and locked-in (or even ill or dead) visitors. He should also be aware of what personnel are working in the building or grounds at night.

It must be emphasized that if one is to have a guard who is efficient and alert, one must be careful in selection, and must pay accordingly, rather than simply hiring someone's aged uncle out of sympathy for him or because he is willing to work for very little. No matter how friendly you or your staff may be, the public generally comes in contact only with your guard(s). If guards are sleepy, senile, or surly, the visitor will take away a rather negative impression of your place. If guards have been well trained, have been indoctrinated with the message of your institution, and are alert, friendly, and obviously trying to help the visitor enjoy his stay, this will also come across. If you want a guard of this latter caliber you must be willing to pay him a living wage, and you must interest him in what the museum is trying to do.

In addition to an alert security staff, there should be liaison with the local police in order that they may be familiar with your layout, and know what are your areas of vulnerability. In the event of riot, for example, how long would it take the law officers to get to your museum? This in an increasing possibility in these times, and one lone guard waving a club or a firearm would probably only aggravate the situation.

Security and alarm systems may be connected to a central guard station within the building, or to the police or state trooper station, according to one's local situation. There are a great many electronic sensing devices, special door locks, and alarm systems available; but in the final analysis nothing is more effective than an alert guard, or a guard with a well-trained dog. Even complex security systems fail for the simple but human reason that the more elaborate they are, the more people place complete faith in them and fail to remain alert. Even the best system can break down occasionally or can be side-stepped by an intelligent professional burglar.

Below are some of the currently available types of alarms, some of which you can install, and some of which need specialized factory installation. If you do install such equipment, remember that the more people who know about it and about where and how it is installed, the less effective it is.

Some Alarm Systems:

Audio-detectors—can be used as check-in stations by guards. Also pick up noises in gallery.

Closed circuit television—only as effective as the people monitoring it. Somewhat expensive.

Door switches—turned on after closing hours to monitor which areas are being entered. Often used with speaker system since employees may be working after hours.

Micro-switches—can be placed under object. Will set off alarm and/or a signal at a central panel if object is disturbed.

Motion-detectors—such as radar units and those based on high frequency sound waves. Show up changes in frequency and cause an alarm as someone crosses their path.

Photo-electric eyes—can be set up in a number of ways. Some types can be by-passed, especially if their location is obvious.

Switches or circuits—around doors, windows, skylights. Can be inactivated by knowledgeable burglars.

In addition to securing your collection against theft and vandalism, consider also the safety of artifacts against accidental damage. Objects on exhibit should be securely mounted so that vibrations, breezes, or sonic booms will not cause them to fall off their mounts. It is often necessary to fasten an object to a wall either for physical security or for design purposes. But avoid drilling, screwing, or nailing into the artifact in order to accomplish this purpose, as it will lessen the value of the object. The well-being of the object is far more important than a dramatic exhibit technique. A simple and harmless clamp or bracket can usually be made of wood, or bent to fit out of brazing rod, scrap metal, or plastic.

Do not place heavy objects on tall, thin pedestals where they can be knocked over easily, possibly injuring a visitor as well as the object. Fragile items or those that are easily knocked over should be behind a barrier or in a corner of a room rather than near doors or entrances or in narrow passageways.

Firearms, knives, lighting devices and other tempting artifacts should be displayed behind glass or other secure barriers.

SUGGESTED READING

Gage, Babcock, and Associates. *Protecting the Library and Its Resources, A Guide to Physical Protection and Insurance.* Chicago: American Library Association, 1963.
Extensive information on physical protection against fire, theft, vandalism, etc., and aspects of insurance.

Keck, Caroline K., et al. *A Primer on Museum Security.* Cooperstown: New York State Historical Association, 1966.
Covers forgery, insurance, environment, theft, and various forms of physical security. *Recommended.*

Lawton, John B., and Block, Huntington T. "Museum Insurance." *Curator* 9 (December, 1966): 289-297.

"Safe Art." *Architectural and Engineering News.* (January, 1967).
This journal is published by Chilton and Company, Philadelphia, Penn. 19139.

Sugden, Robert P., *Safeguarding Works of Art: Storage, Packing, Transportation, and Insurance.* New York: Metropolitan Museum of Art, 1948.

3
Fire Protection

In case of fire: Personal safety comes first!

Have the number of the fire department clearly posted.

Call the fire department and get personnel and visitors out!

If, after having done this, the fire is still small enough that you think you can contain it with an extinguisher without danger to yourself, then you may do so. But do not attempt to fight large fires or to rescue anything; and having once left the building do not go back in.

No matter how small a fire may seem, call the fire department immediately, even if you are sure you can put it out before they arrive. The fire department would much rather roll up when there is no apparent need for them, than to wait until you have finally decided that the fire was, after all, too much for you to handle.

PREVENTATIVE MEASURES

There is nothing mysterious about fire prevention. Vigilance, maintenance of equipment, and good housekeeping can prevent most fires from starting. Have the local fire marshal, fire chief, or a qualified fireman come to your premises and check for fire hazards at least once a year. There may be defective wiring, a leaky chimney, a worn-out heating plant, leaking fuel oil, a custodian's closet full of oily rags, a dirty packing room, or the like. Since about 75 percent of all fires start in winter months, according to the National Fire Protection Association, your heating system should be checked yearly.

If you have remote areas or buildings that are not often visited, it is a good idea to have "fire howlers"—pressure-can alarms with a heat collecting collar that sets off a noise when the temperature at the ceiling goes above a certain level. If your building is large or complex, have occasional fire drills and procedures worked out for personnel. Be sure that you have proper exit signs, panic doors, fire

12

escapes, alternate escape routes, and Jacobs' ladders if necessary. If there are fire hoses in your building, they should be checked periodically for condition. But do not attempt to use them yourself—leave the job to trained firemen who are capable of handling high pressure hoses safely!

FIRE EXTINGUISHERS

Know the location of all extinguishers in your building, and be certain that your personnel do too. Even though they are not attractive, extinguishers should be in plain sight and not discreetly hidden in closets or behind panels. Know in advance each extinguisher's class-rating and how to use it. Do not expect miracles—a 25-pound extinguisher is good for only about one minute of flow. Avoid the obsolete carbon tetrachloride type of extinguisher. When this material is sprayed on a fire it breaks down and forms phosgene, a poisonous war gas. If, in addition, there is heated zinc metal in conjunction with the fire, an explosive compound is formed. Furthermore, the fumes from carbon tetrachloride can cause liver and kidney damage and eventually death. If you have any extinguishers of this type, throw them out! Avoid also beer-can-size aerosol extinguishers. In addition to having a small capacity, they are so cheaply made that they are not dependable, and fire companies warn against placing reliance upon them.

Notice the rating on your extinguishers, and use them only for the proper class of fire:

Class A: Ordinary combustibles, like paper and wood
Class B: Inflammable liquids, solvents, grease, and oil
Class C: Energized electric equipment

A fourth class of fire, which includes burning chemicals and metals such as Dow metal, magnesium, phosphorous, sodium, and potassium, should not be fought by the amateur.

Generally Class A extinguishers are water-based and are operated by any one of a number of mechanisms. Their one drawback in a museum is that the resultant water damage to some types of objects, such as parchment, paintings, and prints, may be as serious as the

13

damage from fire. The potassium bicarbonate-based "dry powder" extinguishers are usually recommended only for B and C class fires, as are the carbon dioxide gas extinguishers. The one type of extinguisher that is suitable for class A, B, and C fires and is harmless to the artifacts is the dry powder type based on monoammonium phosphate. All these types are clearly marked, and your fire department or insurance company or the National Fire Protection Association (60 Batterymarch Street, Boston, Mass. 02110) can tell you where to get further information.

When purchasing extinguishers keep these factors in mind:

1. Don't buy one that is so heavy that women or elderly personnel cannot pick it up.
2. Be sure that you know the company and the salesman who handles the extinguishers. There are many, many "fly-by-night" extinguisher salesmen in the business who peddle an inferior product, or who will not service their product, or who know nothing about it. If in doubt, check with your local fire department officials to see what they recommend; and see whether they will recharge your extinguishers for you for a service fee. Good extinguishers are complex precision mechanisms, so expect them to be relatively expensive.

Remember the sequence in case of fire:

Call the fire department.

Get the people out.

Only fight the fire if it is small and if you do not endanger yourself. Human life is more important than property.

SUGGESTED READING

"Hot, Hotter, Hottest." *The Laboratory* 34:3 (1966).
   A general discussion of newest fire-fighting materials; can be obtained from Fisher Scientific Company, Springfield, N. J.
Jenkins, Joseph, ed. *Protecting Our Heritage: A Discourse on Fire Protection and Prevention in Historic Buildings and Landmarks.* Boston, Mass.: National Fire Protection Association, 1970.

Available from the National Fire Protection Association, 60 Battery-march Street, Boston, Massachusetts, who have a great number of other pamphlets on fire-fighting systems, safety, and protection of buildings, contents, and occupants. It can also be ordered through the AASLH.

SUPPLIES

Fire Extinguishers (A-B-C Class)
   The Ansul Company, Marinette, Wis.
   Swartz Fire Protection Company, 226 North 10th St., Philadelphia, Penn.

Fire Howlers
   Falcon Automatic Fire Detector, Model S-36—Falcon Alarm Company, Summit, N.J.

4
Environment

Control over temperature and humidity, the amount and type of light that comes into the museum, and the state of cleanliness of even the hidden areas of the building are among the most important ways in which the conservator can slow down the deterioration of artifacts. It might seem that some of these problems should be the concern of the custodian or exhibition personnel. The logic of temperature and humidity control, for instance, might be to adjust it to the convenience of the director, or to the comfort of visitors or whoever is closest to the thermostat and feels like changing it. All too frequently control over these factors is just this capricious and arbitrary. It is important to remember that environmental control in a museum is for the protection of the objects rather than for the convenience and comfort of personnel and visitors.

ENVIRONMENTAL PROBLEMS AND SYMPTOMS

Excessively high humidity (over 68%)

Mold growths form on organic materials, wooden objects swell, veneers may peel, oxidation of metals is increased and, in combination with industrial vapors or salt air, degradation of all materials is accelerated.

Periodic, rapid, or long-term fluctuations in humidity from extremes of 15% in winter up to 80% in summer as part of a daily or seasonal cycle, leads to sweating of metal and hard surfaces, flaking and cracking of paint layers, veneers, and marquetry work, and stresses in wooden panels and furniture. Ideally, humidity levels should vary as little as possible the year around.

Extreme heat and/or dryness

Extreme heat and/or dryness (from direct sun, incandescent lamps, radiators or ducts) causes brittleness in paper, leather, and textiles, and shrinking and checking of wood. Frames and joints open up, wood-panel paintings cup and may crack.

16

Sunlight and ultraviolet rays

Bleaching and hardening and deformation result for many organic materials. Embrittlement of paper and textiles, discoloration and increasing insolubility of oils and varnishes can result. Watercolors and some oil colors fade badly; woods may either darken or bleach out. Ultraviolet rays from sunlight or fluorescent tubes combined with heat and/or humidity speed up oxidation and degradation of most materials.

Atmospheric pollution

Sulphur dioxide from coal smoke and some types of oil smoke by itself or in combination with water vapor (forming sulphurous acid) bleaches paper, decays leather, and causes metallic corrosion. Another inimical compound often found in industrial environments is hydrogen sulphide. It blackens white lead (a common paint ingredient), and when combined with moisture and ozone it forms a destructive acid which attacks organic and inorganic materials. Industrial pollution plus gasoline exhaust fumes, can generate methane, propane, acetylene, and any number of other gases, all of which can form endless destructive combinations.

Soot particles and dust in the atmosphere are not only dirty in themselves but form a nucleus for moisture and increased deterioration. Dew (a weak carbonic acid solution) eats away at limestone and concrete, bleaches organic materials, forms a focusing lens for the sun's rays to destroy paint film, and speeds up oxidation of metal. Sea air contains moisture plus salts that bleach paint and organic materials and corrode metals.

Bacterial action

Bacterial action (mold, mildew, fungus, dry rot) takes place when a nutrient material is combined with warmth, high humidity, and weak or non-existing light. Paper is eaten up, or foxing and mold growth occur; starch pastes weaken, causing loss of adhesion. Leather is weakened; and when high humidity is combined with lack of ventilation, leather, wood, and textiles are destroyed. Often metallic corrosion is accelerated, as some bacteria can attack metal.

Climate considerations

Temperate Zone. This is probably the area where the greatest number of museums are found. Although nominally temperate, it has great fluctuation in temperature and relative humidity from one season to another.

Maritime Zone. This is also an area where many museums are found. Although generally more humid than the temperate zone, it has a narrower range of temperature and humidity fluctuations.

Tropical Zone. An area of great heat, high humidity, and seasonal rains, it presents almost impossible difficulties for museums unless they have elaborate air conditioning and give constant attention to collections.

Desert and Sub-Arctic Zones. Although these two areas differ from one another in their average yearly temperature, both represent climates of low humidity and little annual precipitation.

Microclimate. This term applies to the measure of temperature and relative humidity within a limited given area, such as a specific room in a building, a packing case, or an exhibition case. A given area may differ from the rest of a building (or room) by virtue of having more windows, by having a heating pipe pass through it, by the presence of drafty doors leading to the outside, etc. If objects are to be stored in such areas it is important to know how much or how often the temperature and relative humidity vary.

ENVIRONMENTAL CONTROL

Relative humidity

Absolute humidity is the amount of water vapor in a given volume of air. Relative humidity—abbreviated R.H.—is the relationship between the amount of water vapor in the air and the amount needed to saturate that air (100% R.H.) at a given temperature and air pressure. The higher the temperature, the more water vapor a given volume of air can hold. Thus, when the temperature drops, the air is capable of holding less and the moisture will condense on surrounding nonporous materials like metal and glass or will be absorbed by porous materials. On the other hand, air with a low relative humidity will pick up moisture from surrounding furniture, nasal membranes, or other moisture-containing materials. This is why in winter, with hot, dry furnace air circulating, there is a tendency for furniture, prints, and human beings to dry out.

A relative humidity level of 55% represents the ideal for the best protection of woodenware, leather, and parchment. If this is not attainable, the acceptable range falls within not less than 45% and not more than 60%. Whatever your relative humidity is within this range, the important thing is to maintain it with as little daily or seasonal fluctuation as possible. Below 40% R.H., static electricity builds up; paper and some types of cloth stick together; dust and lint become a bigger problem; and organic materials dry out. Over 68% R.H., mold growths are encouraged.

While 55% R.H. represents the ideal, it is difficult to achieve this level in old buildings except at prohibitive cost. During winter months when there is great contrast between the outside and inside temperatures, the recommended indoor relative humidity will cause sweating walls and frozen windows in any but the best insulated buildings. This occurs as the warmer and moister air is chilled by cold walls and panes. For this reason it may be practical to maintain a higher relative humidity only in specific gallery or storage areas by means of portable humidifiers.

Know the rating or capacity of a humidifier. It is useless to expect a single home-type appliance to maintain an adequate humidity level in a large exhibition hall. However, the capacity of uncontrolled humidifiers should always be low in order to prevent too much of a good thing.

Measuring the relative humidity

The measuring device most commonly seen is the "humidity indicator" found in connection with desk or wall sets. These sets usually contain a thermometer, a barometer, and a humidity indicator; and while the first two instruments are relatively accurate, the humidity device may be incorrect by 15% or more. The cheapest devices are cardboard humidity indicators containing cobalt salts which change color in response to R.H. changes, and which have roughly the same accuracy as the previously-mentioned device.

Two accurate though relatively inexpensive devices (about $8-$12) are wet bulb thermometers and sling psychrometers. In both cases one takes the comparative reading between the dry and the wet thermometers, consults a sliding-chart rule, and reads off the R.H. percentage. An aspirating or recording hygrometer can be purchased for $50-$200, but because of budget limitations, most historical societies will find a simple wet-bulb thermometer adequate. Such devices are available from instrument companies and scientific supply houses.

Acquiring humidity control

If you have money and are about to build a new museum building, then of course an air conditioning system with all its implied controls is the ideal. But the cost and the complexity of installing air conditioning in an existing building, especially a historic house, makes it impractical in many situations. Portable humidifiers can provide a solution for specific areas. Either evaporative or spray-type humidifiers may be used. But remember that distilled water must be used in spray-type units. Tap water contains dissolved mineral salts which will otherwise be deposited all over a room. If this seems nit-picking, just look at the limy deposits that build up on the vanes and louvers of the average home furnace humidifier after a long winter.

If the summers are humid, then dehumidifying units can be used, and the water which they condense can be bottled and safely used for the winter humidifying units. But neither humidifiers nor dehumidifiers can do their best work in rooms where there are great numbers of windows or where there is heavy traffic going in and out. Under such circumstances several units will be needed.

For small areas, such as closed cases, humidity control may be acquired through the use of silica gel and various salt solutions which

20

are conditioned to a certain humidity level and installed in a hidden part of the case. (For details of this procedure, see the article by Dr. Nathan Stolow in the bibliography.)

Protecting against light

Ultraviolet light, whether it comes from sunlight or from fluorescent lamps, tends to fade and embrittle organic materials. Heat damage can also result from uncontrolled sunlight pouring in through large windows, from incandescent bulbs in an unventilated case, from fluorescent fixtures if the ballasts are inside the case, or from photographers' flood lights set too close to objects. Therefore, proper lighting, not from the dramatic point of view but in regard to the safety of an object, must be an important consideration.

The human eye has a tremendous range of accommodation, from reasonable comfort in the full glare of sunshine to the ability to pick one's way across an open field by starlight. But because we have become accustomed to high levels of artificial illumination, we tend to feel that it is always necessary. Although high levels of candlepower are not really needed and when incorrectly used can cause eyestrain, the present tendency in exhibitions is to use dramatic lighting with great contrasts. This not only gives the visitor visual fatigue from reaccommodating the eyes, but concentrated sources of light can be detrimental to many classes of artifacts.

Incandescent spotlights generate tremendous heat, particularly in unvented cases. Photofloods, frequently set close to oil paintings for a long period of time while the photographer is making his adjustments, can literally "cook" a painting to death. Fluorescent tubes in themselves are cool; but if the ballasts, which operate at a temperature of about 190°F., are inside the case with the tube, heat build-up can occur. In planning the lighting of exhibits and cases it is wise to pick a bulb of the lowest level that will adequately light the exhibit and to have ventilation at the tops of the cases if possible. This may be done by simply drilling a few one-inch holes which are covered with wire screen; or by installing a small exhaust fan with filters. Budget will determine the complexity of the arrangement.

21

While fluorescent tubes in themselves generate little heat, they are rich in ultraviolet rays that badly affect textiles, paints, dyes, varnishes, and related materials. Plastic sleeves can be obtained to slip over the tubes and substantially reduce the ultraviolet emanations. (See source list, page 24.) They cost about 50 cents a foot for small amounts; but since the filters work indefinitely, they soon pay for themselves in terms of increased life span of the objects. Remember filters will only decrease, but not completely eliminate, ultraviolet rays.

Sunshine has a double hazard of heat build-up plus ultraviolet rays and must be particularly guarded against. The heat not only dries and embrittles objects, but if a large amount of window area is exposed to sunlight, the resulting amount of heat will cause an almost impossible strain on an air conditioner in the warm months. There are a variety of glasses made by such companies as Corning and Pittsburgh Plate which will modify the amount of heat, light, and ultraviolet rays coming through. All of them are rather expensive, but if your exhibition space is limited and items must be shown in southerly exposures, these glasses are a practical solution. Plastic sheets which absorb ultraviolet rays may be placed over existing windows. The UF-1 Plexiglas is clear, while the UF-3 type has a slightly yellow tinge and gives more protection. If all these answers seem too expensive, then consider the alternative of having screens, lined milium drapes (cloth with aluminum reflecting surface), louvers, or venetian blinds in sunlit rooms, and having them drawn during the hot and sunny parts of the day. If your budget will not allow even this modest expenditure, then the only alternative is to keep only metal objects, ceramics, or sculpture in such rooms.

Owners of clothing stores that face south know how quickly sunlight will damage stock that is in the window even for a short time; and they take precautions to use yellow transparent screens and awnings to protect their investment. If you are trying to save the materials of the past for the future, you have an even greater obligation to protect your collections.

Providing clean air

If a museum is located in an industrial area, there is no easy way to produce clean air short of an enclosed air conditioning and filtering system. In the absence of such a system, objects should be stored in closed containers or plastic bags; exhibit cases should be sealed against dust and dirt, and if possible the air should circulate through a filter screen. Periodically do a thorough housekeeping and vacuuming of areas to reduce dirt before it settles on objects. Good housekeeping is an endless chore, but it is still one of the most important facets of good conservation.

SUGGESTED READING

Abstracts: Environmental Effects on Materials and Equipment. Published by the National Research Council, Prevention of Deterioration Center. Section "A" deals with environmental factors, $50 yearly subscription; Section "B" physical and engineering factors, $25 yearly.

Buck, Richard D., and Amdur, Elias J. "A Specification for Museum Air-conditioning and Humidity Control." *Museum News* 43 (December, 1964), Technical Supplement #5.

Emerick, R. H., "Heating of Restorations," *Progressive Architecture.* National Trust Publications #210 (August, 1957).

Feller, Robert L., "Control of Deteriorating Effects of Light Upon Museum Objects: Heating Effects of Illuminating by Incandescent Lamps." *Museum. News* 46 (May, 1968), Technical Supplement.
A very good study on the effect of light, oxygen, and other factors on the deterioration of paint and organic materials, and methods and materials for overcoming it.

——————————. "The Deteriorating Effect of Light on Museum Objects." *Museum News* 42 (June, 1964), Technical Supplement #3.

Fundamentals of Building Insulation. Chicago: Insulation Board Institute, 111 West Washington Street, 1963.

Greathouse, Glenn A., and Wessell, Carl John, eds. *Deterioration of Materials: Causes and Preventive Techniques.* New York: Reinhold Publishing Corporation, National Research Council, 1954.

A complete manual listing causes of destruction of every class of material, and giving preventative techniques.

Harrison, Laurence S., *Report on the Deteriorating Effects of Modern Light Sources.* New York: Metropolitan Museum of Art, 1954.

McCrone, W. C., "The Importance of Thinking Small." In *Heating, Piping, and Air-Conditioning.* New York: Reinhold Publishing Corporation, 1966.

The use of the miscroscope in identifying environmental contaminants.

Noblecourt, Andre, *Protection of Cultural Property in the Event of Armed Conflict.* Paris: UNESCO, 1958.

Part Two—Chapter 2, "Biological Hazard"; Part Three—Chapter 2, "Protection Against Other Hazards"; Part Five—Chapter 5, "Air-Conditioning."

Stolow, Nathan, "Fundamental Case Design for Humidity Sensitive Museum Collections." *Museum News* 44 (February, 1966), Technical Supplement #11.

A short technical discussion of problems and solutions to maintaining environmental stability in a packing case or exhibition case.

SUPPLIES

Humidification Apparatus
> Abrax Instrument Company, 179-15 P Jamaica Ave:, Jamaica, N.Y. 11432
> American Filter Company, 215 Central Ave., Louisville, Ky.
> Armstrong Machine Works, Three Rivers, Mich.

Dry-wet Bulb Thermometers and Sling Psychrometers
> Abrax Instrument Company, 179-15 P Jamaica Ave., Jamaica, N.Y. 11432
> Taylor Instrument Company, Rochester, N.Y.

Cardboard Humidity Indicators
> TALAS—Technical Library Service, 104 Fifth Ave., New York, N.Y. 10011

Light Filters: Plexiglas—U.F.-1 (clear) and U.F.-3 (slightly yellow) to be slipped over fluorescent tubes.
> Glass Distributors Inc., 1741 Johnson St. N.W., Washington, D.C.
> TALAS—Technical Library Service, 104 Fifth Ave., New York, N.Y. 10011

"Solar-Screen"—sold in sheets or ready-made shades in clear or amber, or in liquid form; for cutting down on U.V.

Solar Screen, 12-49 150th Street, Whitestone, New York

Photochromic Glass

A light sensitive glass which will darken or lighten in response to intensity of illumination.

Corning Glass Works Inc., Corning, N.Y.

"Solar-Gray" Tinted Glass

Pittsburgh Plate Glass Company, Pittsburgh, Penn.

5
Packing for Shipment

If you allow artifacts to travel beyond the premises of your institution, then your responsibility for their well-being is not confined to the museum environment. While naturally you cannot guarantee their safety once the objects leave your sight, there are measures by which you can minimize the dangers of travel.

It should be understood at the outset that no matter how carefully one packs objects for shipment, travel automatically means wear and stress to an object, and a shortened life span. Changes of humidity during travel will affect wooden objects, paintings, and leather; and vibration or jarring can dislodge loosely adhering pieces. There is always a possibility that the entire item will be lost enroute through loss of tags, misshipment, theft or vandalism, or through phenomena which insurance companies and shipping firms call "Acts of God." Even if an object reaches its destination, there may be ignorant handling or poor care in unpacking, in temporary storage, and in exhibition mounting. The effect of the damage may not become apparent until several months after the object has come back to the institution.

Having stated these warnings, and accepted the fact that institutions still will send their pieces out on loan, let us consider what can be done to minimize the damage.

EXAMINING BEFORE SHIPMENT

The curator should make a condition check before objects are packed. Do paintings have loose, wobbly frames, bits of broken gesso, any loose or cupping flakes of paints? Are there wires or screw eyes on the back of the frame which can poke holes in the picture packed next to it? Are there fragile pieces of sculpture with "stick-out" parts that need special padding and support? Are wooden objects so weak, worm-eaten, or full of mends that they cannot survive travel? Is the object so sensitive to humidity changes that it might crack or come apart, as is the case with many wooden musical instruments? If textiles are going out, do you know enough about the material and its weight and method of fabrication to know whether it should be folded, rolled, rucked, or creased?

Because human memory is so imperfect, the condition of objects should be recorded on a shipping record sheet before they travel, and ideally photographs should be made. This is particularly important for objects which by nature of their materials and method of fabrication are fragile or vulnerable to shock, breakage, or crushing. For example, stoneware pottery and cast iron are heavy, hard materials, but are quite easily fractured; and even though theoretically one can reconstruct their form from the broken pieces, they are difficult materials to mend satisfactorily. Objects made of more ephemeral materials may be almost impossible to mend without the aid of photos, even if one has all the pieces. As an example, some years ago a Melanesian mask made of bark cloth, cane, and badly worm-eaten softwood came back from loan almost completely crushed. Even though all of the pieces were there it would have been impossible to even conjecture the total form from the broken splints and crumpled bits of bark cloth without the aid of photographs. There is no such thing as having records that are too complete.

Photographic comparisons will also show any alteration in condition which has occurred during the loan period; if the condition existed prior to shipment the borrowing institution will not receive unwarranted blame for it.

PACKING

Since the chore of packing is not considered a white collar job, curators usually delegate it to a man-of-all-work and then forget about it. But it is the curator who is responsible for the care of the collections; and if the packing is poorly done, it is a reflection on the professional ability of the curator and not on the custodian. If the curator is fortunate enough to have someone to do the packing, it is essential that this person be taught the correct way to pack artifacts. The curator must be on hand to examine objects for condition and to oversee packing procedures. If there is an accident somewhere along the line, the insurance company is less likely to charge you with negligence if they know that you have a standard supervised procedure.

Have adequate supplies of dollies, straps, and padding in order to move objects safely. Don't try to carry large, heavy, or awkward items alone; use two or more people for absolute safety both to the object and to yourself. Never, never carry an item when you have screwdrivers, drills, or any tools sticking out of your pockets! Aside from the risks to personal safety, you can damage an object with the sharp instruments.

When you set the object down, look out for sharp-edged items and loose tools, and check for screws, nails, or staples that could get mixed in with the packing materials. Try to have a packing area with uncluttered space to minimize accidents. Ideally it should be easily accessible from the storage area and exhibition rooms, and to the outside loading area. The object should not have to be bumped up and down stairs, nor around sharp corners, nor through swinging doors.

The ideal packing is a "womb within a womb," giving the object maximum cushioning and minimum movement within the case. Small objects should be packed in such a way that they are identified as objects and not thrown away with the packing. To ensure this, make a packing list to accompany each case, identifying the objects enclosed.

Packing and cushioning materials should not stain, discolor, chemically affect, nor soil the objects. For example: vapors from mothballs or crystals in a batch of woolens can soften and melt the tarred center of double-face waterproof paper; excelsior breaks into small messy bits and dust particles; the acetic vapor from new excelsior has been reported as the cause of corrosion in nonferrous metal objects; colored papers, if damp, can cause stains on marble statuary; and inks from felt marking pens can bleed through paper and cause irreversible damage to absorbent objects. Watch out for details.

To prevent penetration of dirt and liquids, line the inside of the case with a tough, waterproof paper that is not in contact with the objects. When travel involves great temperature and humidity changes, the interior of the box should be lined with one or more

Inadequate packing methods resulted in damage to this iron horse in transit. Even the heavy-gauge sheet iron of the tail and the sturdy cast iron of the foot could not withstand shipment when poorly protected.

layers of soft insulation materials to slow down the effects of environmental change. Upon arrival at their destination, the boxes should sit in the receiving area for a day or so before being opened in order to let the objects become conditioned to the new environment.

For maximum safety the objects should not be in an open slatwork crate, but should be completely boxed with a tough punctureproof skin of material like heavy plywood. External braces of 1" x 4"'s not only strengthen the box, but can be used as handholds or skids for awkward or bulky packages. But avoid packing too much weight or bulk in one box—there may be only one elderly person at the receiving end to move it. An exhibit of historic hardware went on tour in New York state a few years ago. Because of the weight of individual crates, a lady who administered a historical society without help was obliged to let the boxes sit on the back steps until time for them to be picked up for the next museum. Not only might the objects have been damaged by rain or snow, but what might have been an interesting exhibit was lost to that town because the "master-planning" of the exhibit did not take into account the limitations of personnel and moving equipment in a small museum.

In making internal braces use screws, not nails, for easy removal and safety to the enclosed contents. Always use screws for the lid. as well. This will minimize vibration and eliminate shocks in opening and closing the case.

When the crate is closed, glue (don't nail or tack) the shipping label and return address to the package securely, and do the same with your re-packing· instructions. Build the best box you can, and pack scientifically—remember that insurance is only a form of compensation and will not replace lost or broken objects.

SUGGESTED READING

Buck, R. D., "Hazards of International Shipment." *Bulletin of the American Group IIC* 6 (May, 1966).

Dudley, Dorothy and Bezold, Irma. *Museum Registration Methods*. Rev. ed. Washington, D.C.: American Association of Museums, 1968.

Keck, Caroline. *Safeguarding Your Collection in Travel*. Nashville, Tenn.: AASLH, 1970.

Michaels, Peter. "Lender Beware." *Museum News* 43 (September, 1964): 11-12.

Sugden, Robert. *Safeguarding Works of Art: Storage, Packing, Transportation, and Insurance*. New York: Metropolitan Museum of Art, 1948.

PRELIMINARIES
TO CONSERVATION

PART

II

In the foregoing chapters we have considered how to provide the kind of environment that will be conducive to the health and safety of historical artifacts. But regardless of the efforts made to ensure the maximum life of objects in your collections, the time will come when more deliberate measures are required to conserve a particular artifact. Knowing the proper first aid that can repair damage or forestall deterioration, and knowing when to call in a specialist to assume responsibility for the conservation of an object, are essential to the well-being of the historical relics in your charge.

Two preliminaries are necessary before proceeding with more specific treatments. The first of these deals with the documentation of the artifact. The following notes on the identification of historical relics will suggest the kinds of considerations that are important in determining the authenticity and value of the item. How can you be assured that the object is worthy of the time and care you are about to invest?

The second preliminary is the creation of the kind of facilities and work area that will permit the proper conservation treatment. Your workshop is the clinical laboratory where you will apply first aid to valuable artifacts, and the care with which you prepare and maintain the workshop will in large part determine the success of your efforts.

6
The Artifact and Its Documentation

Relics of the past are important to the historian in that they reveal something about the lives and attitudes of our predecessors, and they are important to the connoisseur and the scientist for a study of aesthetic values or an understanding of earlier technology. But there is an additional reason why antiquities have value: private individuals enjoy collecting them. And while the number of authentic documents of the past is limited, the number of collectors is growing daily. Since it is obviously a sellers' market, spurious, "improved," and "cheered-up" pieces come to light daily, and it therefore behooves the collector to be careful.

Major or expensive pieces should have good documentation and/or a guarantee from the dealer or seller. Harpsichords and Hepplewhite chairs are not usually found in old barns and sold for a song. Antique dealers out in the country are just as aware of prices as are city dealers, and if they have a good piece it will usually go for a fair market price. Beware of bargains unless you want to be fooled. Your only defense is scholarship and experience; learn all you can about styles, techniques, materials, and tools.

The museum of the past may have been the community attic. But today, with the realization that it has a specific story to tell, with limited storage space, and with its obligation to preserve valid artifacts that it owns, a museum must of necessity be more discriminating in what it accepts.

Not all artifacts can be traced or documented easily, alas, and the curator must often rely on his own background of experience and scholarship in accepting an object as a valid type. For example, some carpenters' tools have not changed shape in the last several hundred years; a traditional type of try square or saw may look much the same whether 50 years old or 150 years old.

If you are interested in an object, but are unsure about its authenticity, there are experts and appraisers who will give you an opinion for a nominal fee or a percentage of the object's market value. Since they are presumably disinterested outsiders, their fee and opinion are usually worth the money.

Museum people, for the most part, are not up on current market prices and fluctuations and should stay out of the appraisal business.

The recommendations you offer might backfire.. If you give an individual an appraisal on a piece he brings in, he may use it as a bargaining price in trying to sell the item to you, or use your quoted figure in trying to sell it to a neighboring museum. If you give a high appraisal for an object which has been donated to you with income tax deduction in mind, are you sure you can back it up with the Bureau of Internal Revenue on the basis of current market prices?

There is no short cut to knowing the real from the spurious. What is necessary is a long apprenticeship in studying old pieces, thumbing through style and hallmark books, having a knowledge of brasses, turnings, carvings, and designs, and a good idea of the technology of the period.

In addition to an object's authenticity and market value, there are other considerations that should be made before you accept a piece. What is the physical condition of the object? Is there enough left to justify its acceptance, and how much would its repair and conservation cost? Is its value historical, aesthetic, or fetishistic? Is this piece really germane to the story your institution is telling?

The following few pages on tools, hardware, and materials may serve as a limited introduction to the problems encountered in identification, and what one needs to know about the materials in his collection.

FASTENINGS

Wooden pins or tree-nails (trunnels) are often considered by the layman to be "old timey" and the crude forerunners of metal nails. Indeed wooden nails and dowels may have come before metal ones, but they also have held their own up to the present in house and furniture construction. Traditional trunnels were irregular looking and roughly octagonal in cross-section, rather than circular as are modern dowels. This is because, contrary to the old saying, square (or at least polygonal) pegs do fit better in round holes than round pegs do. The trunnels were made slightly oversize, so that when driven into a round hole, the shoulders or edges of the trunnel bit into the wood and made a tight fit. They were also made of tough seasoned hardwood, whereas the wood they were driven into was usually greener. As the latter seasoned, it shrank slightly, and held the trunnel even tighter. For this reason pins and joints on houses and well-made furniture did not need glue for tight joints.

The earliest nails and hardware came to America from abroad, but by the mid-1600's production of spikes, nails, brads, and tacks had begun in this country; and by the beginning of the 1800's, the first machinemade nails were being turned out. For a complete chronology of nail types and developments, see the suggested readings; but a point needs to be made about using nails for dating. While machinemade nails first appeared at the end of the eighteenth century, handmade nails continued to be produced and used for specialized purposes much later. Therefore, the presence or absence of a certain type of nail in a piece is not by itself definitive in dating the piece. Machinemade cut nails (or "square nails") are still being produced and a careful examination (using a hand lens if necessary) should be made to tell the difference between them and the earliest machinemade or handwrought nails.

While the principle of the screw has been known from antiquity, it was not until the 1600's that it was used for fastenings. By the 1700's it was used with table hinges, clockwork, and firearms. The slots were irregular, the threads generally coarse, and the small ends were flat. In the early nineteenth century machine-made screws appeared, and by 1846, the modern gimlet-pointed screw. About the same time modern nuts and bolts with standardized threads made their appearance. But because many blacksmiths still had their old taps, hand-made bolts were still made occasionally until quite recent times.

TOOL MARKS

Saws

The traditional two-man pit saw, an enormous handsaw, became obsolete in most areas of the United States soon after the earliest

A few characteristic tool marks:

1. A circle saw.

pioneering days, though its use persisted in England into the present century. To use it, one man stood on top of the log and his mate stood facing him but under the log in a pit. As the cut progressed, the pitman moved closer and closer to the topman until the saw was almost vertical, whereupon both men stepped backwards (away from each other) and the saw assumed an angle again. Thus the pitsaw ordinarily left a very distinctive mark—a series of fan-shaped scars along the side of the plank or board, each individually formed and quite unlike the mechanical regularity of a power saw.

The power-driven up-and-down saw, or sash saw, (a type in which the blade is not under tension is also called a "muley" saw) was the standard sawmill saw until the mid-nineteenth century. It produced a regular pattern of parallel tooth marks, as every tooth went past the plank on every reciprocating stroke. Thus the pattern of marks repeats itself about every half inch or so down the plank. The modern band saw, an endless ribbon of edge-toothed steel, makes a similar mark. However, the "repeats" in the pattern are several inches apart because, due to the great length of the blade, any damaged or odd tooth goes past the plank at widely-spaced intervals. The circular saw leaves a regular series of interlocking curved lines. Since it came into general use in this country about the time of the Civil War, its marks can be used to tentatively date a piece of sawed lumber. But beware: in a few places, circular saws were used quite early, while in a few other places, the old-fashioned "up-and-down" saw was still in operation well toward the end of the nineteenth century. Even the pit saw continued to be used in England into the twentieth century, and a few shipyards in the United States clung to it too. All these saw marks, therefore, are good indicators when used with care and discrimination, but they can be deceptive.

Hand planes

Hand-planed boards are characterized by a series of long shallow concave valleys along their length. Carpenters put a shallow curve on the plane blade in order to eliminate ridges or long scratches which would result from using a square-edged blade to dress rough lumber. One can sometimes see this effect by looking at the surface

36

2. From an old hand plane with its slightly curved edge

3. A shingle which has been split with a froe. Modern ones almost always bear marks of the circle saw.

in a raking light, or feel it by running the fingers at right angles to the grain.

Old augers and drill bits

These tools had a variety of points and cutting edges which have their own sequential development. Persons interested in details of this subject are referred to the books by H. C. Mercer and W. L. Goodman, listed in the suggested readings under "tools."

Axe, broadaxe, and adze-marks, and the study of which tool was used when and how, comprise another entire field beyond the scope of this discussion. However, there is one common bit of folk-lore about adze marks that should be squelched. People sometimes exclaim in delight at "crude adze marks" found on old beams that have been exposed inadvertently—or sometimes purposefully with the intent of "earlying up" the house. Timbers that were meant to be hidden were usually only roughly dressed square with a *broadaxe* since they were to be covered with plaster or paneling. But timbers that were to be exposed were frequently dressed with an adze for a smooth surface. The adze is a finishing and shaping tool and cannot easily be used to remove much stock. Our ancestors did not want a rough-hewn effect; like us, they wanted their homes to look as nice as possible. Timbers meant to be exposed were often so smooth in appearance that unless one ran his hand across the surface, he would think it had been planed.

LUMBER AND FURNITURE

Old lumber can be distinguished from modern by its great variation in thickness of planks and studding. Whereas a modern 2″ x 4″ stud will not vary more than 1/16″ in lumber yards across the country, old wall studding will have a variety of measurements. Old lumber generally has clear grain with few knots in it, and has an even, cloudy, slightly opaque patina that modern oil stains cannot duplicate. Fakers, who sometimes use old pieces of boards to build or "improve" an existing antique, run into difficulty when sawing an old board, since the exposed wood will be a color different from the weathered surface. And since end-grain wood takes stains and dyes so readily, it is almost impossible to "age" the new saw marks to match the old surface.

There are a variety of ways of "distressing" reproductions to make them look old—oil and chemical stains, sulphur and ammonia vapors, pouring burning shellac on a surface, beating the surface with tire chains, strewing on carpet tacks and beating them with a board, rasping edges for worn effect, sand blasting and/or charring and scraping, making shotgun pellet holes, acid burns, and so on—the list of methods is almost endless. The only defense of the museum person is scholarship applied with sharp eyes.

Begin by asking these questions: does the furniture look worn in logical areas? Has the piece been "upgraded" by turnings or carvings which are not germane to its period or type? It has been mentioned before that dating by nails and screws alone is not necessarily definitive because legitimate modern repairs may have been made to the piece, and handmade nails can still be acquired or made in a home forge. In any event, look closely at the nails, screws, and hardware with a hand lens. Check for evidence of corrosion or carbide scale, as well as built-in dirt, varnish, and paint layers, and scratches and scuffs around escutcheons that indicate use. It is often said that the way to tell an old varnish is by its hardness, and an examination of the finish of a piece of furniture may give a clue to its authenticity. But since most modern synthetic varnishes dry fast, and some of them become harder and tougher than some of the old spirit or oil-resin varnishes, this test is not necessarily accurate. Tests to differentiate among various varnishes and their approximate ages are so complex, even for the paint and varnish chemist, that the amateur is warned to place no reliance on "thumbnail tests."

Turn the piece upside-down; open drawers; look at joints, patinas, evidence of tool and scribe marks, and penciled-in or old pasted-on signatures. Even old-looking labels can be counterfeited, or cut out of old newspaper advertisements, so they should not be accepted automatically. Repairs to improve strength are legitimate, as is the addition of some missing parts for stability; but this does not improve the value of the piece. Only original parts are of value to the scholar.

FIREARMS AND POWDERHORNS

Unless you are a real expert in either of these fields do not put out good money for items unless you get a money-back guarantee or a clear understanding of the conditions under which the item has been sold. There is a tremendous market for firearms and their accoutrements; and, unfortunately, there is an equally tremendous number of people piecing together old odds and bits and "improving" existing legitimate pieces with engravings and false signatures. It has been said that if all of "Pancho Villa's pistols" in private collections were assembled together, there would be enough to equip the whole Mexican army. Reputable arms dealers charge a tidy price for their goods; but most of them sell on a basis of "examine it X-number of days, and your money back if you don't like it."

Engraved powderhorns and scrimshaw sell for quite high prices by any standard. But remember, new whale's teeth and cowhorns are easily purchased; and a good engraver with no scruples can deliver almost any scene or map you want. Be wary, and consult experts before you buy. You can make up the lost money; but it takes a long time to get over the sense of chagrin when you have been badly stung. If you find that you have a fake, take it out of your display. in order that a falsehood is not perpetuated. It may seem difficult to do, especially if you have paid good money for the article. Making mistakes is human; but to admit to it and to learn from it is one mark of a professional.

SUGGESTED READING

People in the museum field, and particularly conservators, should know something of the materials, techniques of manufacture, and styles of the past in order to work intelligently with the identification of objects in time and place. A working knowledge of technology of the past will help not only in identification but in detecting spurious or altered pieces.

Scientific tools will help authenticate or disprove only if a person knows what it is he is looking for. The presence of Prussian blue in a painting is of no consequence unless you know when this color came into use or whether its presence is part of the original painting or represents later repair work. Similarly, the presence of "square nails" in a piece of furniture proves nothing about its age since square nails have been made from Roman times up-to the present.

There is no one book or piece of scientific apparatus that will give you all the answers or keep you from being fooled occasionally by a clever fraud. It has been said, "The expert who says he has never been stung is either lying or just doesn't realize it yet." Reading, technical examination, comparison, and handling many pieces are the ways to acquire a body of sound knowledge.

Many well-known books that discuss furniture styles and touch marks in silver and pewter are generally available. The following list of books represents more specialized discussions of the identification and preservation of these and additional kinds of artifacts important to conservationists. Some of the sources discuss artifacts having aesthetic (and monetary) value, such as paintings; others might be called "tin-can archaeology," since the objects *per se* are not valuable although they help to give the scholar information about dating and past technology. This list is only a sampling, and the curator is urged to make his own list as he goes along.

Many articles of value appear in professional journals or in apparently unrelated technical fields, so one should develop the habit of perusing the library's periodical section. In addition, several of the sources in the suggested readings are published by organizations concerned with conservation. UNESCO (Place Fontenoy, Paris 7, France) with its Rome Centre (256 Via Cavour), the International Institute of Conservation (London and New York; see *Studies* below), and the Prevention of Deterioration Center (National Research Center, 2101 Constitution Ave., N.W., Washington, D.C. 20025) are the most important groups. If you examine their publications regularly, you will find much valuable information.

Architectural Restoration

Bullock, Orin M., Jr. *The Restoration Manual: An Illustrated Guide to the Preservation and Restoration of Old Buildings.* Norwalk, Conn.: Silvermine Publishers, 1966.

The hows, ifs, whats, and whys of restoring historical buildings. Heavily illustrated. Chapters on "The Architect," development of programs, selecting the period to be restored, historical research, execution of restoration, specifications, post-restoration maintenance; plus a bibliography, glossary, and appendices with notes on restoration of masonry, heating, etc. This book is a basic part of anyone's library in this field.

Isham, Norman M., and Brown, Albert F. *Early Connecticut Houses: An Historical and Architectural Study.* New York: Dover Publications, 1965.

A reprint of a work of 1900, which gives architectural and construction details of early houses, plus information on stone and brickwork, mortars, framing, clapboarding.

Forgery In Art (Bibliography compiled by Sheldon Keck, Cooperstown, New York).

Coremans, Paul. *Van Meergeren's Faked Vermeers and De Hooghs: A Scientific Examination.* London: Cassell and Company, 1949.

Friedlander, Max J. *On Art and Connoisseurship.* Boston: Beacon Press, 1960.

Kurz, Otto. *Fakes, A Handbook for Collectors and Students.* 2nd ed. rev. New York: Dover Publications, 1967.

Special Issue on Forgeries: The Magazine of Art. New York: American Federation of Arts, 41:5 (1948).

Tietze, Hans. *Genuine and False.* New York: Chanticleer Press, 1948.

Van de Wall, H.; Wurtenberg, T.; and Froentjes, Wiebo. *Aspects of Art Forgery.* The Hague: Institute of Criminal Law and Criminology, 1962.

Furniture

Cescinsky, Herbert. *The Gentle Art of Faking Furniture.* New York: Dover Publications, 1968.

Deals predominantly with fine English and Continental pieces but contains much valuable specific advice and has philosophical approach to knowing furniture.

Marsh, Moreton. *The Easy Expert in Collecting and Restoring American Antiques.* Philadelphia: J. B. Lippincott Company, 1959.

What to look for in old brasses, tool marks, dimensions, and methods of construction. Don't let the somewhat facetious title put you off. This book brings together much valid information.

DOCUMENTATION

General

Barber, J. *Wild Fowl Decoys.* New York: Dover Publications, 1954.

Earnest, Adele. *The Art of the Decoy: American Bird Carvings.* New York: Bramhall House, 1958.

Can you tell the difference between an old decoy and a modern fake? What would you look for?

Evans, Bergen. *The Natural History of Nonsense.* New York: Vintage Books (Random House), 1958.

Has nothing at all to do with fake furniture or old masters; but makes one aware of how easily gulled we are, often because we want to be, and consequently how Cardiff Giants, flying saucers, and Piltdown Man can be perpetuated.

Fall, Frieda Kay. *Art Objects, Their Care and Preservation.* Washington, D.C.: Museum Publications, 1967.

Keck, Caroline K. *A Handbook on the Care of Paintings.* Nashville, Tenn.: American Association for State and Local History, 1965.

Peterson, Harold L., ed. *Encyclopedia of Firearms.* New York: E. P. Dutton and Company, 1964.

Section "F," "Fakes and Forgeries," contains valuable information for the budding arms collector. This is a real "caveat emptor" field, in which abound many self-confessed experts who often have the morality of a pirate.

Plenderleith, Harold J. *The Conservation of Antiquities and Works of Art: Treatment, Repair, and Restoration.* London: Oxford University Press, 1956. Later reprints are available.

Contains information throughout on how to set up and carry out various conservation projects, plus supplementary tables and information in the appendix. Number *one* on your purchase list.

Rath, Frederick L., Jr., and O'Connell, Merrilyn R. *Guide to Historic Preservation, Historical Agencies, and Museum Practices: A Selective Bibliography.* Cooperstown, N.Y.: New York State Historical Association, 1970.

Recent Advances in Conservation, Contributions to the IIC Rome Conference, 1961. Edited by Garry Thomson. Washington, D.C.: Butterworths, 1963.

In addition to specific articles on conservation, contains articles on the training of conservators, which will give the amateur or part-time conservator in a small museum an idea of what is required to become a competent professional.

Studies in Conservation, Abstracts, IIC News. Published periodically by the International Institute for Conservation of Historic and Artistic Works, 608 Grand Bldgs., Trafalgar Square, London, WC 2N, 5HN, England.

This is the organization to which most professional conservators belong. If you wish to keep abreast of developments in the field, it will be worth your while to join and receive their publications. Subscription and membership inquiries should be directed to the above address.

Synthetic Materials Used in the Conservation of Cultural Property. Rome: Rome Centre of the International Center for the Study of the Preservation and Restoration of Cultural Property, 256 Via Cavour, 1963.

Historical Archaeology

Fontana, B. L. "Bottles, Buckets, and Horseshoes, The Unrespectable in American Archaeology." *Keystone Folklore Quarterly* 13 (Fall, 1968). A good general summary of the problems of identifying recent historical material. Excellent bibliography; published by Point Park College in Pittsburgh and the Pennsylvania Folklore Society.

Hagerty, Gilbert. "The Indian Trade Knife in Oneida Territory." *Pennsylvania Archaeologist* 33 (July, 1963). Stylistic traits of knives traded to Eastern Indians during contacts in the early historical period. Illustrated. Published by the Society for Pennsylvania Architecture, Aliquippa, Penn. 15001.

Heizer, Robert F., ed. *The Archaeologist at Work: A Source Book in Archaeological Method and Interpretation.* New York: Harper and Row, 1959. An important source book on archaeological techniques and interpretation covering a wide range of topics: "The Identification and Interpretation of Strata," "Excavation of a Virginia Burial Ground in 1784," "Plant Growth as Indicators of Buried Features," "Paleolithic Housing," etc.

———————————. *A Guide to Archaeological Field Methods.* Palo Alto, Calif.: National Press, 1966. Contains a list of materials needed for field conservation techniques; valuable for the section on dealing with skeletal material.

"Indian Trade Guns." *The Missouri Archaeologist* 22 (December, 1960). Extensive articles (illustrated) on early firearms traded to Indians; detailed chronology of parts and tools used by gunsmiths of the period. Obtainable from the University of Missouri at Columbia.

"Johnny Ward's Ranch," *The Kiva* 28 (October-December, 1962). Here's a real sleeper! An account of the excavation of a ranchhouse site. It is not only a manual of "tin-can archaeology" (recent historical archaeology), but it contains research in areas untouched by most scholars, such as *new* material on development of various kinds of nails, chronology of such things as milk cans, sardine tins, brass cartridge types, bottles, hardware, and shoes. Anyone involved in working on nineteenth-century sites can use this to good effect. Published by the Arizona Archaeology and Historical Society, Arizona State Museum in Tucson.

Petersen, Eugene T. *Gentlemen on the Frontier,* Mackinac Island, Mich.: Mackinac Island State Park Commission, 1964. A photographic survey of materials of a mid-eighteenth century fort and trading post. Contains a cross section of civilian and military goods, but is especially strong in pictures of buttons, rosaries, and baling seals.

Peterson, Harold L. *American Indian Tomahawks.* New York: Museum of the American Indian, Heye Foundation, 1965. An illustrated chronology of Indian tomahawks, both for warfare and ceremony, plus "Squaw's hatchets," and comparative military and carpenter hatchets of the eighteenth and nineteenth century. Since trade hatchets are frequently mistaken for tomahawks, this book should help clear the air.

Woodward, Arthur. *Indian Trade Goods.* Portland, Ore.: Oregon Historical Society, 1967. Identification and dating of many items; especially good on buttons and trade beads.

Marine Archaeology

Holmquist, June D., and Wheeler, Ardis H., eds. *Diving Into the Past: Theories, Techniques, and Application of Underwater Archaeology.* St. Paul, Minn.: Minnesota Historical Society, Conference on Underwater Archaeology, 1964.

A good pioneer work on techniques, legal ramifications, and problems of this branch of archaeology, of interest to the historian as well. The sections on historical research and identification and conservation of artifacts are particularly recommended, as they contain material not usually covered. Extensive bibliography.

Peterson, Mendel. *History Under the Sea: A Manual for Underwater Exploration.* Washington, D.C.: Smithsonian Institution Press, 1969.
A handbook on underwater archaeology, with a section (illustrated) devoted to the problems and solutions of conserving materials from a marine environment. Since underwater archaeology is becoming increasingly popular, the conservator in a historical museum should know something about the special techniques involved in· salvaging these materials.

Tools

Batcheler, Penelope Hartshorne. "Paint Color Research and Restoration." *History News* 23 (October, 1968), Technical Leaflet #15, rev. ed.
Information on how to determine· the original colors of a building.

Goodman, W. L. *The History of Woodworking Tools.* New York: David McKay Company, 1966.
Gives an understanding of what tools were used and when, particularly various types of drills and bits.

Hodgkinson, Ralph. "Tools of the Woodworker: Axes, Adzes, and Hatchets." *History News* 20 (May, 1965), Technical Leaflet #28.
Characteristic shapes of these tools, and their markings on wood.

Hommel, Rudolf P. *China at Work.* Doylestown, Penn.: Bucks County Historical Society, 1937.
Details of existing primitive tools and their techniques.

Hummel, Charles F. *With Hammer in Hand: The Dominy Craftsman of East Hampton, New York.* Charlottesville, Va.: University Press of Virginia, for the Henry Francis du Pont Winterthur Museum, 1968.

Mercer, Henry C. *Ancient Carpenter's Tools.* 3rd ed. Doylestown, Penn.: Bucks County Historical Society, 1960.
Note: The Bucks County Historical Society also puts out a reprint of one of Mercer's early monographs on the dating of old houses which contains a section on nails, hinges, etc.

Nelson, Lee H. "Nail Chronology as an Aid to Dating Old Buildings." *History News* 24 (November, 1968), Technical Leaflet #48.

Discussion (and illustrations) of development of nail types and how they overlap in time.

Welsh, Peter C. *Woodworking Tools*. Washington, D.C.: Smithsonian Institution Press, Paper #51, 1966.

7
The Workshop and Its Use

This discussion of furnishings and tools is addressed to the person who will probably be doing some elementary conservation as a part of his duties in a small museum or historical society. Even though lacking scientific training, a person who takes the time to study the books listed in the bibliography and who proceeds slowly and methodically can do an important job of conserving collections. Care and restraint are more important than specialized scientific apparatus, which are only expensive toys if one does not know how to use them or to interpret the results. Most of the apparatus and supplies suggested here are relatively inexpensive and can be added to the workshop a bit at a time, as one has use for them, or as the budget dictates.

The most important things are (a) to work only to the limits of your understanding; (b) to have systematic procedures; and (c) if you find yourself beyond your depth, admit it, and make use of specialists to help work out your problem.

THE WORKROOM

There are a number of ideals for a good workroom; but probably number one for efficient work is an area in a quiet part of the building, away from the main line of traffic, casual visitors, and staff coffee-klatches. Interruptions lead to distraction, which in turn leads to mistakes.

Lighting

Preferably the room should have adequate natural light, plus windows that can be opened to assist in the ventilation of fumes. General lighting today is usually obtained from fluorescent lights; but check before you purchase your lighting tubes. All of the major companies put out several shades of "white," ranging in tone from icy blue to rather pinkish yellow. You may wish to purchase combinations of these tones in order to have a comfortable, reasonably color-corrected light. Most local dealers will carry only a "cool daylight" tube; but if you insist you can obtain what you want. One or two small flexible table lamps will be handy for concentrated or raking light. These range in price from about $15 to $25. Two

47

photoflood bulbs plus reflectors and tripods will help in doing record photography. An infrared bulb will be useful for heating or drying objects; and. an ultraviolet examining lamp will occasionally be needed in examining the fluorescence of certain adhesives or varnish coatings. A mercury-vapor type costs about $75; but less expensive fluorescent tube types are available for around $20.

Try to have as many electrical outlets as possible at regular intervals around the room, plus a few supplementary heavy-duty extension cords with double plug-in outlets attached. But be careful where you put them; few items are as annoying and dangerous as extension cords trailing all over the lab floors. All plugs should be of the modern three-wire grounded type.

Tables

Examination and work tables are probably your most important tools. Until you have decided your requirements in height, overall dimensions, and shelves, your best bet is to start off with a temporary table, made from a flush door or a piece of 3/4" x 4' x 8' plywood mounted on trestles. Your final main worktable .should be free standing so you can have access to it from all four sides, and it should be 3 to 4 feet wide, depending on your reach, so you can handle large mats and textiles. If your work area is limited, you may also want to have the table on rollers or casters for the most flexible use of the existing space. The area under the table can be utilized for shelves, racks, and drawers for storage of tools, paints, paper, and other supplies. But plan enough knee space, so you will not be obliged to sit sidesaddle when you are seated at the table. The surface of the table can vary, but many conservators working with hot materials find that a hard heatproof table surface like "Transite" lowers fire danger and is easy to clean.

In addition to the main table, which is used for examination, cutting paper, working on textiles, and general light duties, there should be a heavier workbench for hammering, sawing, and general rough work. This should be set in a separate area where sawdust, filings, and dirt will not contaminate other materials. If at all possible this area should be partitioned off, and if necessary an auxiliary ventilating fan installed. A large tank-type or shop vacuum cleaner used after every dusting, filing, or sawing operation will also help to reduce the dirt hazard.

Sink

A sink or washbasin with drainboards is essential for any small workshop. If your local water supply is heavily contaminated with sulphur, chlorine, or minerals, you may find it necessary to purchase a water softener or distilled water for critical work. If you occasionally need a large wash container, and a big sink is prohibitively expensive or space-consuming, you can improvise by making a wooden box to the required size and lining it with heavy-duty polyethylene sheeting; or make a more permanent one by lining the box with fiberglass cloth cemented down with epoxy resin.

Be careful what you pour down the sink! Plaster of Paris and many fillers and adhesives can set up in the pipes or traps, creating a tidy-sized plumbing bill. Solvents left in the trap and not well flushed down with water and detergent can create a pocket of explosive fumes.

Workroom storage

Storage should be adequate, not only for paper, chemicals, tools, and supplies, but also for the various objects that are undergoing treatment. Since many of these objects are valuable, it is important that the room be secure. Can the doors and windows be locked against easy outside access by thieves or vandals?

EQUIPMENT

Optical devices

Binocular

A binocular magnifier which fits over the head and comes in a variety of low magnifications sells for about $15. Even at this low price the optics are relatively good; and it has the further advantage that you can wear your prescription glasses under it. A binocular

49

(or stereo) microscope is a rather sizable investment, about $400 or more. Cheaper ones are available, but their optical systems are poorer. It is better to use the inexpensive headset lenses and save your money for a first class stereo-microscope than to compromise on a mediocre one.

Monocular

Monocular loupes can be purchased from jewelers or opticians in various magnifications. One type fits against the eye socket; other types fit over one's glasses or can be permanently attached to them. These sell for $3-$5. Hand lenses or linen-tester lenses range from $3-10; or you can purchase a large combination reading glass with a built-in fluorescent light source mounted on a flexible stand for about $35.

Using Magnifying Devices

For ease in working use the lowest practical magnification. You will have a greater depth of field—that is, the objects will not go in and out of focus so quickly—and you will see a wider area of material. With higher-powered lenses, focusing is more critical; you see a smaller area; and the apparent motion or trembling of tools or probes under the lens is greatly exaggerated. When working with lenses for any period of time, the eyes tend to tire rather quickly. If you are using monocular devices learn to keep both eyes open to prevent squinting and discomfort. Before looking up from an instrument, close your eyes for a few seconds as you raise your head. Then focus on something at the other end of the room for a short time before you resume your work at the lenses. These tricks will help prevent eyestrain or nausea.

Poor lenses will be fuzzy at the edges, distorted, or colored, and will make your work difficult. You have only one pair of eyes, so always buy the best lenses you can possibly afford.

Heating devices

A Bunsen burner or a gas ring, an adjustable electric hotplate, and an alcohol lamp will probably serve most of your needs. If

Various types of magnifying devices are available. Buy the best quality you can afford.

critical temperature controls or a higher heat is needed, suitable devices are available from scientific supply houses. Be sure when ordering a Bunsen burner that you get one with the proper orifice— one adapted to the type of gas available in your area. Be sure, too, that you comply with all fire laws and insurance requirements in the installation of naked-flame devices.

Balances

Unless you are doing micro-chemical work, an inexpensive set of student-grade balances sensitive to 1/2 gram will probably meet most of your needs. You can also have them graduated in ounces; but the metric system is the one most used by scientists and conservators. Student balances usually range from $25 to $40.

Using Weighing Devices

A slight digression at this point may be in order to explain the making of solutions of various percentages. When adding a *solid* to a *liquid* (for example, washing soda to water) measure the weight of the solid and add enough liquid to make the required amount. For example, to make 1 liter solution of 5% washing soda, weigh 50 grams of soda, and put in a graduated container, and add enough water to make 1 liter. (1 gram of solid is equal in weight to 1 ml of water). Incidentally, the terms cc (cubic centimeters) and ml (milliliter) have the same meaning, though ml is more commonly used at present.

When adding a *liquid* to a *liquid* (for example, hydrochloric acid to water) measure *volume* for *volume*. Although liquids do not all have the same specific gravity (weight per volume), the usual practice outside of exacting analytical laboratories is to assume that they do have. Thus, to make 1 liter of a 5% solution of hydrochloric acid, add 50 milliliters (ml) of concentrated acid to 950 ml of water.

If you do not have metric measures you can use the avoirdupois measure, based on the assumption that a pint of liquid weighs 16 ounces. However, it is more difficult to determine exact percentages of solutions since 16 ounces divided into 100% gives odd fractions. For example, adding 1 ounce of acid to 15 ounces of

51

Have an assigned place for all your tools, such as this tool board. Outline a position for each tool so you will know at a glance which ones are missing.

water gives a 6 1/4% solution. To make one-pint solution of 5% hydrochloric acid, 4/5 ounce of acid must be added to 15 1/5 ounces of water, which is a bit awkward to guess accurately. Therefore, for those who at present cannot afford metric balances and graduates and who may be using kitchen scales and Pyrex pint measuring cups, I suggest the rough and ready convention that 1 ounce of chemical to 15 ounces of water equals a 5% solution; and 1 1/2 ounces of chemical to 14 1/2 ounces of water equals a 10% solution.

Hand tools

It is impossible to second guess someone else's tool needs. Whether you buy a $5 handsaw or a $200 radial saw depends on your manual skills, experience, and budget. Just make certain in selecting a tool that it is of the best quality you can afford. Cheap saws and chisels are not worth the effort of sharpening.

Once you have obtained your tools, keep them clean, sharp, and tight in the handles. A hammer head that comes adrift on the down stroke is a dangerous projectile. Screwdrivers cannot work if their edges are gnawed and rounded. Get enough variety of sizes in screwdrivers that you don't "butch" the screw heads. Just wait until you try to remove a "butched" screw. And don't dump all the tools indiscriminately into a tool box—that is the best way to chip chisel and plane blades. Have special drawers, racks, or boards for your tools so you know where they are or whether they are missing. If certain tools are constantly being borrowed by other individuals, get them a set of their own. If you lend out your tools, especially drill bits and chisels, you have only yourself to blame if all your time is spent at the sharpening stone.

Note of caution: be careful of power tools and leave them alone if you are not familiar with their operation. An eye patch or a stump does not increase your working efficiency. Spring-loaded tools like Yankee drills are also dangerous and can gouge artifacts as well as flesh.

Equipping your workshop will be a never-ending process. To keep abreast of available tools and products, get on the mailing lists of chemical and scientific supply houses, craft and art suppliers, and paper suppliers. If you don't know who they are, leaf through copies of technical publications, craftsmen's magazines, and homebuilders publications. Try to plan your needs for some months in advance, both to get a better price on a bulk order, and because some outfits will not ship less than a certain minimum order.

Also, subscribe to technical publications, such as those of the IIC (International Institute of Conservation), the American Association for State and Local History, and other professional organizations. Build up a library of recommended works on paints, carpentry, conservation, light, and related subjects. These books usually run to small editions and are often expensive, but they are among your most valuable tools in the long run.

SAFETY

Throughout this section I have tried to stress the necessity for safety when working with tools, solvents, chemicals, open flames, and electricity. In addition to heeding these precautions, however, it is absolutely necessary to check with your insurance agent, your fire department, and state board to be certain that you are complying with *all* regulations as to the use of certain apparatus or the storage of inflammables. This is especially true when working in an old historic house which may be a firetrap. Carelessness or ignorance will not excuse a heavy fine, cancellation of insurance, nor loss of collections. In some states the regulations are not so strict if you call your work area a "shop" or "studio" instead of a "laboratory," but whatever the safety regulations are, comply with them.

Fire extinguishers

Fire extinguishers in the workroom should be of the A-B-C class, like the newer types of dry powder extinguishers. On *no* account use the carbon tetrachloride type. The fumes are often more toxic than those of a chemical or grease fire. Keep the extinguisher where you can get at it (near a doorway), have it checked periodically for pressure, and be sure it is a brand your local fire department or a reliable salesman can re-charge for you. Part I of this handbook

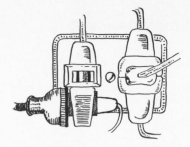

includes additional information about the selection and use of fire extinguishers.

Electricity

Don't overload your lines with more electrical appliances than can be handled safely. If you keep blowing fuses, check with an electrician. And don't give house-room to cheap light-duty appliances, or apparatus with frayed or broken wires. Electrical fires are no fun to fight.

Burners

If you have Bunsen burners or other naked-flame devices, be sure that they are installed in accord with local regulations, are situated away from burnables and are turned off (including pilot lights) when sprays or solvents are in use.

Garbage cans

These should be large (shop-size) of metal, and have close-fitting lids for the safe disposal of oily rags, solvent-soaked cotton, and papers. Empty cans daily if possible. A fire-retardant type is suggested in the supply list.

Safety goggles

Choose either the plastic full-face mask, or the type which fits snugly around the eye sockets, or the gas-proof variety, depending on your needs. Don't work without them, whether you are pouring acid or using an electric drill. You have only one set of eyes!

Safety apparel

Rubber or insulated gloves, aprons, and lab coats save wear and tear on your street clothes and your skin. They are cheap insurance.

Deadly materials

Flammable materials such as chemicals, paints, adhesives and solvents in excess of immediate needs should be stored in fireproof lockers, and "No Smoking" areas should be set up and adhered to where needed. Again, be sure you comply with laws and insurance rules. Keep a poison chart in your lab so you will know what to do or what to tell the doctor in an emergency. Keep acids or alkalis separate from one another so that in the event of breakage or spillage there is not a strong reaction. Strong oxidants, like potassium permanganate, and percussion-sensitive materials, like potassium chlorate, should be handled with due regard for their hazards. Don't play "the boy chemist" and mix materials if you do not know exactly what reactions will result. A helpful book in this respect is the *Manual of Hazardous Chemical Reactions 1968* (NFPA #491M), available from the National Fire Protection Association, 60 Batterymarch Street, Boston, Massachusetts 02110. It is a well-indexed book that describes the violent reactions that can occur when certain chemicals are brought together. Since the potential reactions of many common chemicals and materials may come as a surprise to you, this book is well worth consulting before you embark on an experiment that has not been documented.

Acid solutions

A warning about pouring acid solutions: *do not pour water onto liquid acids* like sulphuric, nitric, or hydrochloric acid or you will have acid spitting up in your face or on your clothes! Pour the required volume of acid *slowly* into the water, a little bit at a time. A considerable amount of heat is given off, enough to break an ordinary glass jar. It is better to mix the liquid in a container of teflon, polyethylene, or in other acid-proof containers available from chemical supply houses.

The same warning applies when adding caustic soda (sodium hydroxide) to water. Add this alkali only a little bit at a time, and feel the side of the container from time to time to be sure the solution is not heating up too fast. Strong alkalis like caustic soda and caustic potash can eat your skin before you know what has happened.

In short, don't take unnecessary risks with strong acids and alkalis.

Ventilation

You must have adequate ventilation if you are working with

solvents, chemicals, heat, and vapors. If you cannot afford a factory product, a local tinsmith should be able to make you a fume hood; the fan can-be purchased through a local electrical contractor. But be sure that it is big enough to draw all the smoke or fumes you will create, and that it is sparkproof. Don't take a chance on working in an unventilated room; the accumulated fumes can lead to explosions, chronic illness, and even death.

RECORDS

Keep full records of all the work you do, no matter how obvious a given procedure may seem at a given moment. Records are vital to good conservation practice, to your own growth as a professional, and to the people who come after you. Among other things, documents and photographic records prevent misunderstandings with directors, patrons, or donors, who all have short memories and may choose to dispute what the condition of the object was before you received it or worked on it.

Your own memory is not infallible either—so *as you proceed* date and document your work on a work sheet that can be typed up later for formal records or insurance reports. When using an adhesive, cleaning solution, or coating (especially patented products), write down as exactly as you can the specific description of the materials used. The person who may later be obliged to take apart a decoy duck that you glued together may have some difficulty working out a solvent if you have only specified "Lok-Tite Miracle" adhesive. That product may no longer be on the market, or the formula may have changed. Specifying that the adhesive was a synthetic resin soluble in acetone or denatured alcohol not only appears more professional but it is considerably more helpful.

Keep a record of your trials and failures, as well as your successes in conserving objects. A record of what did not work in a certain instance may save you time when working on the next object of similar materials.

Keep photo records of your work before, during, and after treatment. What kind of camera you use may be based on your budget or your own preference, but be sure that it is a camera capable of taking close-up views and details of objects if necessary. A blurred box-camera shot taken three feet away is seldom helpful for record purposes. If possible, learn to develop your own negatives. The average photo processing plant does not bring out the best in negatives; and if you have good ones done on fine-grain film, they can be enlarged in printing to bring out whatever details you wish to show.

Among your records you should also keep a file on whatever cameras, optical equipment, or tools you buy, including pertinent warranties, serial numbers, or instruction sheets. It may save you grief when the article needs repair work or new parts.

SUGGESTED READING

"A Conservation Workroom." *Intermuseum Conservation Association Newsletter* 4:2 (1966).
A listing of the conditions, furnishings, tools, and supplies needed for setting up an arts conservation workshop. This newsletter can be obtained from ICA in Oberlin, Ohio.

Coremans, Paul. "The Museum Laboratory." In *The Organization of Museums: Practical Advice: Museums and Monuments* 10. Paris: UNESCO, 1960.
A general survey of the functions of a museum lab and the various techniques by which materials are examined for age, condition, and authenticity.

Organ, R. M. *Design for Scientific Conservation of Antiquities.* Washington, D.C.: Smithsonian Institution Press, 1968.
Complete and current advice on setting up a laboratory for care of artifacts. Covers physical layout, arrangement of furniture, plus a description of tools and equipment and their use. Highly detailed and specific. Although meant for large institutions, even a small museum will find much useful information. Recommended.

UNESCO. *Source Book for Science Teaching.* Paris: UNESCO, 1962.
While this book was published for the teacher working in poor countries with the expectation that he or she would be obliged to make

scientific apparatus out of scrap material, this same situation may apply also in small museums. Thus the section on how to build balances and other lab equipment out of junk will be particularly helpful. Also, included are a variety of work notes, tables of weights, and a host of useful information.

UNESCO. *The Conservation of Cultural Property With Special Reference to Tropical Conditions: Museums and Monuments* 11. Paris: UNESCO, 1968.

While this volume is concerned with conservation under tropical conditions, it contains so much valuable information that anyone will profit by it. The chapters on equipping and setting up a laboratory are particularly useful. *Highly recommended.* Number *two* on your purchase list.

Wheeler, Mortimer. *Archaeology from the Earth.* Baltimore. Md.: Penguin Books, #A 356, 1964.

Contains information on the interlocking role between the archaeologist and conservator, setting up a lab in the field, and the equipment and supplies needed, plus specific methods for treating material.

SUPPLIES

Art Supplies

A. I. Friedman, Inc., 25 West 46th St., New York, N.Y.

Arthur Brown and Bros. Inc., 2 West 46th St., New York, N.Y.

Dick Blick, Box 1267, Galesburg, Ill. 61401

Joseph Mayer Company Inc., 5 Union Square West, New York, N.Y.

Leo Robinson Inc., 42 West 57th St., New York, N.Y.

Phillip Rosenthal and Company, 840 Broadway, New York, N.Y.

Utrecht Linens Inc., 33 Thirty-fifth St., Brooklyn, N.Y.

Chemical and Laboratory Equipment

City Chemical Corporation, 132 W. 22nd St., New York, N.Y.

DuPont Co., 350 Fifth Ave, New York, N.Y. 10001

Fisher Scientific Company (offices nationwide), main office: 52 Fadem Rd., Springfield, N.J. 07061

Shell Chemical Company, Box 831, Pittsburgh, Calif. (waxes, adhesives)

Sonneborn Chemical and Mfg. Corp., (Petroleum Specialities Division) 205 East 42nd St., New York, N.Y. (Micro-crystalline waxes)

Union Carbide Chemical Company, 270 Park Avenue, New York, N.Y. 10017 (polyethylene glycols, emulsions, detergents, poly vinyl acetate)

Scientific Products, 1210 Leon Place, Evanston, Ill. 60201

Heating Elements

Rigid or flexible. Watlow Electrical Manufacturing Company, 1376 Ferguson Ave., St. Louis, Mo.

Hot Air Blower

Up to 500° F, or uses ambient air temperature. Fisher Scientific Company (offices nationwide). Around $40.

Inexpensive Vacuum Apparatus (filter pump)

"Airejector." Fisher Scientific Company. Around $5.

Plastic Boxes and Trays

Althor Company Products, 2301 Benson Avenue, Brooklyn, N.Y.

Poison Chart

Buy one from a chemical manufacturer and study it, *underlining* the hazardous chemicals you use most.

Portable Work and Tool Table

A Sears and Roebuck enameled steel utility roller kitchen table can be modified and utilized quite easily.

Readers, Magnifiers, Binocular Microscopes

Bausch and Lomb Optical Company, Rochester, N.Y.

American Optical Company, Instrument Division, Buffalo, N.Y.

Rubber Aprons, Rubber Gloves, Safety or Fume Proof Glasses

Chemical supply houses, such as Fisher Scientific or Denver Fireclay Company.

Technical Photographic Supplies, Equipment, Problems

Eastman Kodak Company, 343 State St., Rochester, N.Y.

Ultraviolet Lamps

Strobolite Company, 75 West 45th St., New York, N.Y. Long-wave model between $25 and $100.

Ventilating Fans and/or Fume Hoods

Through local electrical contractors or scientific supply houses.

Waste Bin—Flame Retarding (from 3 gal. to 55 gal. capacity)

Laboratories Supply Company, P.O. Box 332, East Station, Yonkers, N.Y. 10704

Work Lights

Incandescent, fluorescent, "Tensor," spark-proof, according to your needs almost anything is available today, and color-controlled if neccessary.

Work Table

Building it to your own specifications is easiest—from wood and adjustable patented slotted metal strips. (Dexion: from Dexion, Inc., 39-25 62nd St., Woodside, N.Y.)

Specialty Tool and Supply Companies

Adjustable Clamp Company, 417 North Ashland Ave., Chicago, Ill. "Pony Clamps," "C" clamps, mitre clamps, etc.

Albert Constantine & Sons, Inc., 2050 Eastchester Rd., New York, N.Y. Woods, hardware, finishing materials, and tools for the cabinet-maker, upholstery tools and materials, and decorative veneers, inlays, and marquetry.

Allcraft Tools & Supply Co., Inc., 215 Park Ave., Hicksville, N.Y. 11301 Tools, metals, findings and supplies for jewelry, silversmithing, and enameling.

Anchor Tool & Supply Company Inc., 12 John St., New York, N.Y. Hand tools, especially for jewelers, metal workers, leather workers, and jeweler's findings.

Craftsman Wood Service Company, 2727 South Mary St., Chicago, Ill. Woods, brasses, hardware, and tools for cabinet makers.

The Craftool Company, Wood-Ridge, N.J. 07075 Presses, tools, supplies and papers for the graphic arts field.

Laboratory Supplies Co., Inc., P.O. Box 332, East Station, Yonkers, N.Y. Makers of "Flame Tamer Waste Receptacle."

Frank Mittermeier, Importer, 3577 East Tremont Ave., New York, N.Y. Wood carving tools, rasps, oilstones.

Sculpture Associates, 101 St. Marks Place, New York, N.Y. Tools and supplies for wood, clay, and stone sculpture.

Woodcraft Supply Corporation, 71 Canal St., Boston, Mass. 02114 Wood carver's and wood worker's chisels and planes, plus specialized wood worker's hand tools, many of which are otherwise unobtainable in the United States.

FIRST AID FOR ARTIFACTS

PART III

Having prepared ourselves with at least the fundamental equipment for practicing conservation, we are now ready to consider some specific problems in treating historic artifacts. Keep in mind these principles no matter what materials you are working with: know as much as you can about the object, identify the problem and the required treatment, plan ahead thoroughly, and proceed cautiously. Remember that we are discussing first aid, not major surgery—when a project is likely to take you beyond the scope of your experience and knowledge, admit it, and call in a specialist.

8
Paper

Until the mid-nineteenth century, better quality European papers were made from clippings of new linen and cotton rags—although old rags, canvas sails, and pieces of rope and netting were also used, and if well washed and processed could be made into stable papers. But with increasing literacy and greater paper consumption, the search for substitutes for cotton and linen rags led to the development of wood pulp-based papers.

Because of the layman's lack of understanding of their varying composition, wood pulp papers have had an undeservedly bad reputation for deteriorating. Paper is basically a compacted mass of cellulose fibers; and the source of cellulose (linen, cotton, jute, straw, hard or softwood, etc.) is not so important to the quality of the paper as the type of processing. Papers of wood pulp base may vary in quality from weak, short-lived newsprint to durable ledger papers suitable for archival work and record storage.

Raw wood contains cellulose, hemi-cellulose, and lignin, in addition to various tannins, gums, oils, and resins. In ordinary softwood mechanical wood pulp, used for newspapers, toilet paper, and builders' wallboards, the wood is simply ground up in water and all these ingredients are left in. This gives a higher yield than does chemically treated wood pulp; and in the case of construction and insulation board, results in an inexpensive and reasonably durable product. But while lignin acts as a binder and strengthener in composition board, it is acidic; and papers made from mechanical pulp are weak, brittle, and short-lived. However, pulp can be treated chemically to acquire the properties desired. Semi-chemical pulp, made from hardwood that has been treated before grinding, has a much lower lignin content than mechanical pulp, and can vary in quality from coarse cardboard to reasonably good quality white paper. Chemical pulp has been cooked with certain chemicals that break down lignins and other materials. This results in an almost pure cellulose. Each of three basic processes—soda, sulphite, and sulphate—has its advantages, depending on such factors as what kind of wood is available, what percentage of yield is necessary, or what properties are wanted in the paper—softness or hardness, absorbency, wet strength, transparency, etc. Since no one method will give every type of paper,

Paper documents improperly mounted: masking tape has come loose, tearing off edges of document; insects have penetrated, eating bits of paper; and the use of cheap acidic matting and mounting board has resulted in stained and weakened documents.

fibers from various processes are often combined to formulate a paper of specific qualities.

PROBLEMS WITH PAPER AND RELATED MATERIALS

1. Excess wetness leads to weakened adhesives, water stains, blurred inks and paints, mold growth, or expansion of dimension. If wetness is combined with heat and agitation, pulping of the paper results.

2. Dryness, heat, and sun cause brittleness, fading, and rapid oxidation.

3. Soot and dirt cause primary staining, and act as a focal point for infection by micro-organisms and foxing.

4. Silverfish, bookworms, crickets, flies, rats, and mice cause dirt and the eating away of covers, bindings, adhesives, and paper.

5. Improper materials: pressure sensitive tapes cause permanent stains; staples and pins cause rust stains and tears; matboards with mechanical pulp wood centers, backings of cheap cardboard or wood paneling cause stains, acid migration to the print, and embrittlement of the paper; acidic pastes cause deterioration of paper; rubber cements cause permanent stains.

6. Carelessness in handling can cause any combination of the above mentioned problems in addition to tearing and wrinkling.

PRIMARY CARE OF PAPER

Many of the threats to paper and related materials can be avoided by primary preventative measures. In addition to the general principles discussed in Part I, follow these additional practices for your paper articles:

1. Avoid exposure to fluctuations in relative humidity, which results in cockling or buckling. (About 30% R.H. is considered ideal.)

2. Avoid constant exposure to light, especially sunlight and fluorescent light, both of which are strong in ultraviolet rays, and cause fading and brittleness.

3. Avoid dampness, especially with coated or enamel finish papers

64

As a result of poor mounting, this document was quite badly embrittled and fell into pieces upon being removed from the mount.

which will stick together.

4. Store documents and prints flat rather than upright, and in proper cases or boxes to keep edges from being torn, frayed, or bent.

5. Check the storage area periodically for insect infestation, and keep the area dusted and vacuumed.

CORRECTIVE MEASURES FOR PAPER PROBLEMS

Bends and wrinkles

First remove pins, staples, and clips. Then put the paper in a relaxing chamber. This need not be anything fancier than a large, reasonably airtight box with space at the bottom for a couple of shallow saucers of water, and a tray above the saucers for the paper. After the paper has stayed in the chamber overnight, or long enough to pick up enough humidity to become limp, it may be ironed smooth under a piece of clean blotting paper, or put through a mangle between two pieces of blotting paper, or simply put between two blotters with a flat weight on top.

Water-soaked papers

If you have a number of documents which are soaked and you cannot get to them all at once, put them in your deep-freeze. This will stop further water damage until you can deal with each one as above.

Insect attack

Use DDT spray, sodium fluoride, or moth crystals.

Foxing and mold growth

Brush off mold with a soft camel-hair brush; expose the paper to a few hours of sunlight and fresh air; and be sure that your storage area has adequate ventilation and less than 60% R.H. The documents may also be sterilized with fumes from thymol crystals. In a tight box mount a 40-watt bulb, and above it put a dish of thymol crystals. Adjust the distance so the dish receives enough heat from the bulb to cause the crystals to evaporate. When you get a pungent gas that smells like "Listerine" the heat is just right. Put the documents inside in a tray, several inches above the dish of crystals, and seal the box for 24 hours or more. The mold will be killed.

Stains

A dry eraser-powder like "Opaline" (available at art supply houses) will remove most dust and dirt stains and grease spots. Pencil marks may be removed with an art gum eraser, *if* the paper is strong enough to stand any abrading. Support the paper when erasing in order not to cause tears or wrinkles, and work carefully.

Many prints and documents may be cleaned by immersion in water. But DO NOT immerse coated papers, parchment or vellum! Before immersing, test the inks and pigments to be sure they will not run, blur, or fade out. If there are pencil marks to be removed, do it before immersion, as a water bath tends to set them. A water bath will often remove many flyspecks, spots, waterstains, and wrinkles. Always support the paper from below by a piece of plastic screening or a sheet of glass. When the paper is removed it should be put between blotters and ironed dry, or dried under weights.

Do not attempt to bleach out spots and stains. Spot bleaching or overall bleaching is only for professional paper conservators. Unless you know what you are doing, you will weaken and degrade the paper, bleach the print to a stark-staring white, fade out color areas or change their value, or create worse water stains than you started with. Be content to remove whatever stains you can safely handle with a water bath.

"Scotch-tape" Stains

Sometimes pressure-sensitive tapes and their adhesive may be removed if treated by a mixture of 1 part acetone, 3 parts alcohol, and 3 parts of toluene (flammable), but it will not remove the brownish stain with any certainty. This is one of the reasons that the use of pressure-sensitive tapes is discouraged.

Candle Wax

These stains can usually be removed with mineral spirits or paint

Knowledge of methods of early paper-making help the conservator understand the causes of and cures for deterioration.

thinner after the heaviest part of the wax has been carefully scraped off with an artist's spatula.

Oil and Grease

Remove by swabbing with a bit of cotton wool soaked in acetone.

Tears

If the tear is ragged, be sure that the edges are aligned back together carefully. A thin needle probe may be used and the fibers teased out a bit to overlap one another. Then apply a minimum of rather stiffish wheat paste with a fine artist's brush, and put a piece of blotter on both sides of the mend. Put the mend under a smooth flat weight for a minute. Remove the blotters and replace with fresh blotters and put the weights on again. This should be done at five-minute intervals for the first half hour or so to be certain the blotters do not stick to the paper. After about an hour, wax paper can be put between the blotters and the mended paper and left under weights overnight. When removed the next day, the mend should be inconspicuous and there should be no cockling of the mended area.

If you have a clean knife-cut with no edges that can be teased together, you will need to paste a thin patch of Japanese tissue (available from Technical Library Service) on the back side. Follow the same blotting and drying procedures described above. Do *not* use pressure-sensitive tapes! A highly recommended cold water paste is Schweitzer's No. 6 Dry Wheat Paste (also available from TALAS: Technical Library Service).

Lamination is sometimes advised for repairing torn and frayed documents and books, but it must be done by specialists. The document is reinforced by having a thin sheet of Japanese tissue applied on each side with thin cellulose acetate film as the adhesive. This must be done under heat and pressure using specialized equipment. If a book is to be treated, it must be taken completely apart first, and afterwards carefully re-bound, an expensive procedure. In addition many documents are acidic and must be deacidified before laminating. Some documents may be in such condition that it is not practical to deacidify them. Again it should be stressed that choosing

67

the answers and carrying out such a process are problems for specialists with the proper training and equipment. The addresses of two recommended firms are listed on the source page. Home lamination kits, which are usually films of pressure sensitive materials, are dangerous to the life of documents and should under no circumstances be used. If you feel that a document or print needs lamination, have a professional do it.

MATTING, MOUNTING, AND FRAMING

Check your collection of old watercolors and prints and see how many have wooden backings—and note how many of these have the impression of the knots and grain working through the back of the paper. Not only is this type of stain almost impossible to remove, but it causes embrittlement of the paper. Replace all wood and corrugated board with neutral rag board mountings and backings, and do it soon.

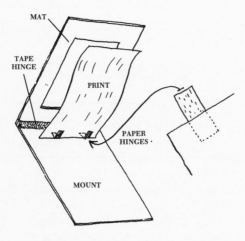

Matting a Print

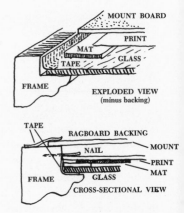

Framing a Print

Backing, mounting, and matting boards must be made of high grade acid-free cardboard stock, or of 100% pure rag board. Cheap matboard, corrugated board, and the like are too acidic.

Hinges for the paper support should be made of Japanese tissue or fine acid-free paper. No sticky tape of any sort! The hinge paste should be a neutral wheat (or other starch) paste which is acid free. Sticky tapes, dry-mounting tissue, and rubber cement are not only difficult to remove, but can cause permanent stains on the print.

The glass and the backing should be sealed with paper tape or pressure-sensitive tape to prevent dust, contaminated air, or moisture from penetrating.

Do not mount a print or watercolor directly against glass; but use a mat or other separating strip. In the event of condensation of moisture within the glass, the print will become spotted and/or cockled.

For prints and maps up to 2′ x 3′, single strength glass is usually sufficient. In larger sizes, double-strength glass is needed. Or you can buy the more expensive but light and shatterproof material, Plexiglas, particularly desirable if the items travel frequently. But one word of warning: do not use Plexiglas over charcoal or pastel drawings. This material is electro-static, and tends to pick up particles of pigment.

When shipping glassed prints or paintings, cover the glass with a crisscross of masking tape to prevent glass from flying around in the event of breakage. But, do not let the tape lap over on the frame. It can, under certain conditions, lift up bits of paint or gold leaf.

SUGGESTED READING

Paper Care

Barrow, W. J. *Manuscripts and Documents, Their Deterioration and Restoration.* Charlottesville, Va.: University Press of Virginia, 1955. Out of print, but well worth the reading if you can obtain a copy.

Cockerell, Douglas. *Bookbinding and the Care of Books.* 5th ed. London: Pitman Publishing Company, 1962.

Cockerell, Sidney. *The Repairing of Books.* London: Sheppard Press, 1958.

Grove, Lee E. "The Care of Paper," *Museum News* 42 (October, 1963): 15-20.

Horton, Carolyn. *Cleaning and Preserving Bindings and Related Materials.* 2nd ed. rev. Chicago: American Library Association, 1969.
Highly recommended—the most helpful and clearly written book yet published of practical advice to the novice. Illustrated.

Kathpalia, Y. P. "Hand-lamination with Cellulose Acetate." *American Archivist* 21:3 (1958): 271-75.

Kane, Lucile M. *A Guide to the Care and Administration of Manuscripts.* 1st ed. rev. Nashville, Tenn.: AASLH, 1966.

Lydenberg, Harry M., and Archer, John. *The Care and Repair of Books.* Revised by John Alden. 4th ed. rev. New York: R. R. Bowker, 1960.

Minogue, Adelaide E. "The Repair and Preservation of Records." *Bulletin of the National Archives* #5 (September, 1943).

"Paper." *CIBA Review* #72 (February, 1949).
Journal of the Society of Chemical Industry in Basle (Switzerland). Can be obtained in the U.S. from CIBA Co. Inc., New York, N.Y.

Rogers, Jerome S., and Beebe, C. W. *Leather Book-bindings and How to Preserve Them.* U.S. Department of Agriculture Leaflet #398. Washington, D.C.: Government Printing Office, 1956.

Tribolet, Harold W. "Rare Book and Paper Repair Techniques." *History News* 25 (March, 1970), Technical Leaflet #13, rev. ed.

——————————. "Trends in Preservation." *Library Trends* 13:2. Published by the University of Illinois Graduate School of Library Science, Urbana, Ill. 61801.

Weidner, M. K. "Damage and Deterioration of Art on Paper Due to Ignorance and Use of Faulty Materials." *Studies in Conservation* 12 (December, 1967).
Published by IIC, London, England. An excellent general survey, with examples of the problems of prints and documents in museum collections resulting from negligence and improper mounting and matting materials.

Wilson, William K., and Forshee, B. W. *Preservation of Documents by Lamination.* National Bureau of Standards Monograph #5. Washington, D.C.: Government Printing Office, 1959.

Framing

Banks, Paul. "Matting and Framing Documents and Art Objects on Paper." Chicago: The Newberry Library, 60 W. Walton, 1968.

A practical 6-page leaflet, plus bibliography and supply sources.

Heydenryk, H. *The Right Frame: A Consideration of the Right and Wrong Methods of Framing Pictures.* New York: J. H. Heineman, 1963.

_____. *The Art and History of Frames.* New York: J. H. Heineman, 1963.

Two books dealing with types of frames desirable for pictures or prints of various periods, plus material on the relationship of the frame to the size and subject of the pictures and the size of the room or gallery. Philosophical rather than "do-it-yourself" in approach.

Ivins, William M., Jr. *How Prints Look: Photographs with a Commentary.* Boston: Beacon Press, 1958.

How to tell a woodcut from a mezzotint.

Watrous, James. *The Craft of Old Master Drawings.* Madison, Wis.: University of Wisconsin Press, 1957.

A very good work which explains the various techniques, tools, and materials of old prints and drawings. Explains graphically and is well illustrated. Gives one a good idea of the nature of the materials he is working with.

SUPPLIES

Acid-Free Wood Pulp Paper

TALAS—Technical Library Service, 104 Fifth Ave., New York, N.Y. 10011.

Recommended source for book presses, brushes, knives, paper, adhesives: all sorts of supplies for paper and book repair work.

All-rag Museum Mat Mounting Board (2 ply and 4 ply)

Andrews-Nelson-Whitehead, 7 Laight St., New York, N.Y. 10013; Charles Bainbridge Sons, 12-26 Cumberland St. Brooklyn, N.Y.; Flax Company, Chicago and New York.

Cellulose Acetate Lamination Service

The Arbee Company, Inc., Central Ave., Stirling, N.J.; W. J. Barrow Research Laboratory Inc., Virginia Historical Society Building, Richmond, Va.

Pest Control

Dekko Silverfish Paks (Insecticide) General Pest Service Company, 2015 Pontius Ave., Los Angeles, Calif.

Thymol Crystals (for killing mold growths), Fisher Scientific Company (offices nationwide).

Japanese Tissues (For mending paper)

TALAS—Technical Library Service, 104 Fifth Ave., New York, N.Y. 10011

Aiko's Art Materials Import, 714 North Wabash, Chicago, Ill. 60611

Leather Preservatives and Potassium Lactate (for preventing acid leather decay)

TALAS—Technical Library Service, 104 Fifth Ave., New York, N.Y. 10011

Paper Cleaners

Wallpaper cleaner takes off dust (but not grease) and can be obtained from paint and decorator stores.

"Opaline" Dry Cleaning Pad, which removes both dirt and grease, is available from TALAS—Technical Library Service, 104 Fifth Ave., N. Y., N.Y. 10011

Phloroglucinol Solution (for testing for lignin in paper) Fisher Scientific Company (offices nationwide)

9
Wood

A living tree may contain up to twice its dry weight in the form of free water which is carried upwards along with dissolved nutrient minerals through tube-like vascular bundles. After being cut down, the tree gradually loses this free water in the tubes, but still contains residual moisture in the cell walls. When the moisture content of the wood is finally at a level of equilibrium with the local environment, the wood is considered to be seasoned.

As wood seasons the amount of shrinkage is greatest in the tangential direction, less in the radial direction, and very little along its length. (Fig. 1) Traditional craftsmen understood this; and consequently timbers, planks, and clapboards were usually sawed or split parallel to the axis of the grain (Fig. 2). Because in cleaving, the line of the natural fiber of the wood was followed, this technique resulted in pieces that had little tendency to crack or warp and that were strong for their given dimension. The modern parallel-sawing technique (Fig. 3), which does not take grain structure into account, utilizes most of the wood. But except for the few center slices, the boards tend as they dry to warp more severely in proportion to the distance from the center of their original location in the log.

PROBLEMS IN WOOD CONSERVATION

Because even seasoned wood responds to varying humidity levels by dimensional changes, it is futile to attempt to close cracks or flatten warped pieces by force. The use of weights, clamps, or glue may effect a temporary success, but if the stresses are still in the piece, they will manifest themselves somewhere else, creating an even worse problem.

One of the major causes of damage to wooden objects is transportation from one climate to another, subjecting the piece to a whole series of thermal shocks and extreme humidity changes en route. It is little wonder that loan objects frequently come back with popped veneer, flaking gesso, cracks, or loose parts. Wood that has reached a working equilibrium in its own environment will react whenever it is subjected to sudden temperature or humidity changes—much to the distress of the lender or borrower.

73

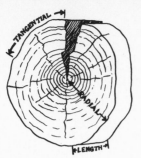

Fig. 1. Tangential, radial, and length directions of wood.

The problems of conserving wood thus resolve themselves into two main concerns: (1) Did the original craftsman understand his material and work with it intelligently? If not, there is not much one can do to compensate for it. (2) Has the object been maintained in a suitable environment? This means not only proper temperature and humidity, but protection from damage by fungi, insects, fire, water, and vandalism.

The job of the conservator of wood, then, concerns itself with this last category—to compensate for the effects of the previous lack of care, and to provide a proper environment for long-term protection.

MAINTAINING THE STABILITY OF WOOD

A relative humidity level of 50-55% is considered ideal for wood, though many small museums cannot afford the equipment to maintain this level constantly. Still many old pieces have come down to us intact that obviously never enjoyed the luxury of this consistent humidity level. What is almost as important as the relative humidity level is a slow and limited change of humidity through the seasons rather than abrupt changes. When there is air conditioning intended only for human comfort, and it is turned off at night, the objects suffer *more* than if they were to remain stored in a barn. Under conditions of extreme dryness and heat, such as an uninsulated attic, wood will survive but will shrink, crack, or check, and glued joints will fail. The wood may also become brittle and darkened. Wood stored in basements that are damp and airless is attacked by fungus growths that can cause dry rot and breakdown of the finish and of the glue. Wood that is subjected to alternate wetting and drying, with little circulation of air, will rot in only a few years. This is why many mortised joints, parts of pilings, and ship bodies "between the wind and the water" are areas of constant trouble. Paint, oil, or varnish alone are not cures for this problem—only adequate air circulation helps. This is demonstrated by surviving seventeenth and early eighteenth-century houses constructed of unpainted wood, but constructed in a manner allowing adequate air to circulate to all parts.

74

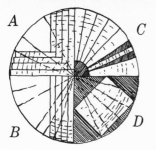

Fig. 2. Quarter- or rift-sawn boards were cut parallel to the grain and had little tendency to warp. Method A gave maximum production but was tedious; Method B turned out fewer but wider boards; Methods C and D produced boards with little tendency to warp but were wasteful of wood.

In short, to preserve wood, maintain adequate ventilation with little or no humidity change; and don't send your prize pieces out on loan. Even if the borrowing institution is in your own aréa, the shock of going from a warm storeroom into an ice-cold van or out in rainy weather may be enough to damage the piece.

CORRECTIVE MEASURES

Warping and splitting

Some causes of warping and splitting have already been discussed. Assuming that a piece has been well made originally, another cause of warping can be the fact that only one face of an object—such as a table top or a sign—has been waxed or painted, allowing a different rate of reaction to humidity change for the two sides. A variety of remedies have been tried: steaming and clamping the piece, painting or waxing the other side, nailing or screwing on wooden or metal clamps or reinforcing strips; or making a series of parallel saw cuts on one side to relieve the stress.

Some of these methods work sometimes; some are tricky or even dangerous to the object, and none is guaranteed. For the most part it is better to leave the piece as is than to damage it forever. Beware of the amateur furniture restorer; if you want a perfect-looking piece, buy a reproduction. Another "cure" widely touted for warping and cracking is the liberal use of "nourishing oil." It may be a commercial or home-made product of such nondrying oils as olive oil or lemon oil, and/or a slow-dryer such as raw linseed oil plus waxes. When one sees how quickly these oils are absorbed into the wood grain, it does seem that they should work. But to be effective these oils should replace the lost moisture, not in the vascular bundles where they are soaked up, but in the cell walls. It is the loss of the so-called "water of impregnation" in the cell walls that causes shrinkage. A perusal of the pertinent literature on experiments in this direction will suggest that the molecules of these various "nourishing oils" are too large to penetrate the cell walls. Experiments are continually being made with various water- and alcohol-soluble

75

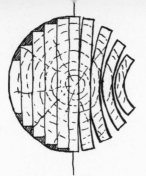

Fig. 3. Parallel- or slash-sawing, the common practice today, results in almost no waste. But the farther from the center a piece is cut, the greater the tendency to warp and twist.

materials that give promise of eventually replacing this lost moisture and stabilizing old pieces permanently; but nothing definitive has been developed as yet. In the meantime, any finish for wood must be regarded as primarily cosmetic rather than "nourishing."

Insects and fungi

Warning: Before mentioning various methods of treatment it must be stressed that all insecticides, fungicides, and fumigating materials are toxic. Some, like HCN (hydrogen cyanide gas), are fatal after just one whiff, while many of the phenol compounds can cause death by being absorbed through the skin. Even the so-called "safe" ones can accumulate in the system over a period of time and cause kidney and liver damage and eventual death.

Good artifacts are worth protecting; but so is your life. Before painting, dipping, spraying, or gassing be sure that you know the properties of the materials you are handling. If you are not certain, hire a professional pest control service. Remember, too, when handling artifacts that have been treated, that many insecticides are residual. Wash your hands after handling such objects.

Insect Fumigants

Cyanide gas, methyl bromide, or carbon disulphide can be used on mixed materials like painted or overstuffed furniture that cannot be safely or easily penetrated by powders or liquids. Fumigation should be done only by professionals, as all these gases are highly toxic, and carbon disulphide is also explosive. In addition, the fumigation may have to be repeated a number of times to be sure that the offending bugs have been eliminated completely. Some types are not knocked out by gas at the egg stage, and since these gases have no residual effect, it is important to know the life cycle of the insect involved.

Combination Insecticides and Fungicides

These materials are often based on chlorinated phenols in a petroleum solvent or aqueous mixtures of metallic salts like zinc or copper. They serve the dual function of preserving wood against fungi such as dry rot and of killing insect life at any stage of the

76

life cycle. These preservatives are residual, give long-lasting protection, and may be dipped, sprayed, or painted on. *Creosote* is the most effective wood preservative known; but it stains wood a black color, leaves a slightly oily residue, smells strong, and irritates human tissue. Therefore, its use in museum work is limited to specialized cases. *Petroleum solvents with penta-chlorophenol or copper naphthenate* may be obtained in different solvent grades. The inexpensive grade stains slightly and is slow to evaporate. The better "water-white" grade does not stain, dries quickly, and can be painted over. But be sure to test the piece to be treated to be certain that the solvent will not damage gilding, varnish, or polychrome on the object. *Water solutions of various metallic salts* are inexpensive and effective, but should not be used on fine objects because of the possibility of swelling and distorting the wood.

Rot and insect damage

Cleanliness, ventilation, and periodic inspection are the best preventatives of rot and insect damage. Preserving dips should be used before trouble starts; end-grain pieces, joints, water-line, and underground areas should be particularly well saturated with preservative. Drip caps and flashing should also be used where needed to be sure water does not settle behind boards and walls of buildings, nor soak into vertical pieces like sign posts and totem poles.

Dead-air areas should have improved ventilation to be sure that fungi do not have a favorable situation. Once dry rot has started, not only the infected wood but the area around it needs to be removed in order to ensure the safety of the rest of the piece. Major surgery on a valuable piece is not only expensive, but also removes original material. For this reason, particularly in marine environments, preventative maintenance is the only practical answer.

There are wax baths and resins that can be used to infuse wet, rotten, or weak wood, killing harmful organisms and returning some mechanical strength and dimensional stability. Some of them are expensive, time-consuming, complex, or require specialized equipment. But because many organic materials which turn up in archaeological and marine sites are in a degraded condition and must be salvaged for scholarly purposes, it is well to be aware of current techniques of consolidation. The function of a consolidating agent is to give mechanical strength and dimensional stability to an artifact. It may act as a bulking agent and/or adhesive, or be used to remove water from the object. Only a generalized description of consolidants is included here, and readers are referred to the bibliography for more specific directions.

Water-logged Wood

The problem is to remove the water by drying processes that will not cause cracking, twisting, or shrinkage. This may involve special drying processes or the replacement of the water by an impregnating material that will strengthen the wood and give dimensional stability. There are a number of factors which determine the condition of wet wood: was it buried in mud, in salt or fresh water, in acid bogs or alkaline soil? Has it mineralized, or been in close contact with certain metals? Has there been extensive leaching of cellulose? What species of wood is it, and what is its porosity? From these questions it is evident that no two wooden items will react the same way to a given treatment.

Various methods are currently in use for treating water-logged wood:

Freeze-drying—The object is frozen and the ice is sublimated out in a vacuum chamber. Much used for biological specimens. Expensive and complex.

Alcohol-ether-resin—Water is removed by a series of baths in ethyl alcohol followed by baths in diethyl ether, which may have resins added to stabilize it. Or the ether may be evaporated in a vacuum. Expensive, and dangerous because of ether fumes that may explode.

Slow-drying—Object is covered with wet sand and wet sacks and gradually dried out over a long period of weeks or months. The surface may have a final finishing coat of some synthetic resin, like epoxy. This treatment is used mostly for large objects such as dugout canoes.

This wooden dipper cracked because it was made of unseasoned wood.

Alum—The object is placed in a hot bath of a saturated solution of potassium aluminum sulphate and water and heated for a number of hours. Upon removal of the wood from the hot bath, the alum crystallizes, having replaced the water in the object. The surface may be given a coating of glue, varnish, or resin. Inexpensive and generally good for large, solid objects, although occasionally there is twisting, or cracking of the surface.

Gelatin-tannin—The object is soaked in an aqueous solution of gelatin, followed by an alcoholic solution of tannin, which is said to harden the gelatin and render the object stable.

"Arigal-C"—A two-part formaldehyde melamine resin. A water-soluble soft resin is put in the bath water, followed by another material which hardens it chemically. This has worked well with small objects. In the event of failure, however, the process is non-reversible.

Polyethylene glycols (also known as P.E.G.)—Water-soluble waxes with a variety of melting points which are used in water baths to replace the water in the wood. Starting with weak solutions the amount of wax and temperature are increased gradually until the water is gone. The waxes of lower molecular weight (P.E.G. 1000-1500) seem to be somewhat sensitive to high humidity and hot weather; but appear to be easy (relatively) to apply. The higher molecular weight (4000) may be used in water or alcohol solutions, and is more resistant to heat and humidity; but it generally requires more sophisticated apparatus and controls to be used successfully. The widely varying physical conditions of pieces of wet wood has resulted in apparently conflicting reports on the efficiency of this treatment, but it seems obvious that this method has a real future. Glycols will, however, soften painted surfaces.

Wax-resin mixtures or microcrystalline waxes—this treatment has been used both for dry, wormy and wet, weak wood. The object is simmered in the wax mixture until the moisture is driven off and bubbling ceases, impregnating the specimen and killing any harmful organisms. This method involves temperature controls and fire safety controls, and polychrome objects must be tested to see whether the heat involved may soften the paint. Unpainted wood treated by this method often turns quite dark and shiny, which may be aesthetically objectionable.

Dry, Weak Wood

In addition to the wax-resin mixture just mentioned, these treatments have been used on dry, weak wood:

"Xylamon-LX-Hardening"—a product which is soluble in turpentine and claimed by its users to be a good, easily penetrating consolidant. This gives strength to an object and presumably can be dissolved out again if desired.

Shellac in alcohol—has been used as a consolidant for dry, weak wood. The alcohol penetrates quite well; but there is some question as to how much of the shellac penetrates, or how much of it migrates out again as the alcohol evaporates. The alcohol will often swell or soften painted objects.

"Git-Rot" and "Calignum"—These are two American two-part resins used for consolidating punky, dry-rotted, or worm-riddled wood. They are non-reversible, cannot be redissolved, and are quite expensive. They work well, however, and are available at marine supply houses.

REFINISHING AND CLEANING WOOD

Stripping down and refinishing old pieces of furniture for fun, profit, or self-instruction may be great sport, if the pieces are your own. But you have no right to play games with furniture or polychrome figures that belong to your institution. This prohibition extends not only to yourself but to local furniture restorers or other craftsmen. They might do a good-looking job of stripping and repainting, but when the piece comes back it will have lost some of its validity as a document of the past. Removing layers of overpaint and salvaging what is left of the original paint calls for a professional conservator who has had years of training, and who understands the chemistry of the solvents and oils involved. Many of the alcohols

Seasonal temperature and humidity changes caused the severe cracking of this wooden statue.

and petroleum based solvents can ruin varnish or paint layers if their gelling, leaching, swelling, or solvent action is not well understood. In addition, there are hazards posed to health from the indiscriminate use of these solvents. All of the foregoing may sound discouraging to the novice and it should; refinishing *is* complex!

Paint strippers made from an alkali base—most notoriously lye—have not only the foregoing disadvantages, but in addition they degrade wood fibers and permanently change the color of some hard woods. Your best job in conservation can be done by staying within the limits of your capability and understanding.

Loose joints

If you want to do a good job of regluing loose joints, be sure that the old glue is thoroughly scraped off both surfaces. New glue does not stick well to old glue. The looseness or snugness of the joints will determine what kind of adhesive you use, as will the finish of the surrounding areas and the species of wood. See the appendix on adhesives for more specific details on suitable glues. If the joints were not originally glued, but were held together by pressure of wedges or force-fit, it may be possible to tighten them by use of a swelling agent. There are alcoholic solutions of glycols such as "Chairloc" which seem to do an effective job. But be sure the "Chairloc" does not get on a painted surface, since it softens some paints.

Dents, scratches and nicks

Sometimes the crushed wood can be swollen up to the original surface by the use of steam. The usual method is to put a few layers of wet rag over the dent, and apply a hot soldering iron one or more times. Keep the pad of wet rags as close to the size of the dent as possible, since the steam may blanch a varnished surface which then may need to be refinished.

Scratches and nicks can usually be filled in cosmetically. Heated stick shellac smoothed into the void is the traditional remedy; but this is not always easy for the novice. There are any number of stains, colored putty sticks, and crayons on the market, which although not

81

so strong and hard as shellac, will do an adequate covering job. These materials are available at most hardware and lumber dealers.

Alligatored and checked finishes

Quite common on old buggies and piano tops, they are a result of either improper drying of the original layers or of breakdown due to age. There are any number of proprietary and homemade solutions for filling in or "re-forming" the finish. Any of these are temporary answers at best and no true solution to the problem. Here you must decide whether you will live with it as is or have the piece refinished, which will be a major undertaking.

Fogginess, milkiness, rings

The treatment depends on the finish. If it is a shellac surface, a rag slightly dampened with alcohol will usually even out the marks; or else a thin shellac solution—1 part of white shellac to 5 parts of alcohol—may be tried. A varnish or oil finish may be compounded out of a variety of drying oils and resins, so the answers will be empirical. A fine abrasive like 0000 pumice or rottenstone in a vehicle like olive oil or slow-evaporating mineral spirits may do the trick; but results are not guaranteed.

Using waxes and shellac

Do not wax directly on raw wood; first use a sealer of dilute white shellac (1 part of 4-pound cut shellac to 3 parts alcohol). Otherwise the old wax accumulates in the pores and is almost impossible to remove. Avoid trying to seal *any* wood with raw linseed oil, which remains sticky almost forever, and picks up dirt from the air.

As for waxes, you may use beeswax dissolved in turpentine, or good commercial paste waxes made of carnauba or candelilla wax ("Butcher's wax" is an example). If desired, a small amount of oil tinting color may be added to give a proper hue. The important thing is to put the wax on in thin layers, and buff thoroughly between layers with a wool cloth or a sheepskin. Do not use liquid self-polishing waxes, as some of them impart a milky surface to the finish.

Shellac is not only a handy sealer for any raw wood, but it is especially good for coniferous woods, as it prevents resin stains from coming through. It is important, however, to dilute shellac, as it drys better and quicker than if used full strength. Do not keep shellac for more than a year, as old shellac has a tendency to remain sticky. Even if you have a can half-full, throw it out if it is old. Your time is worth more than the price of a small can of shellac.

Sanding

If old paint or varnish must be sanded off, use the cheapest grade of paper (flint paper) since the paper soon loads up and must be thrown away. In any sanding operation always sand *with* the grain rather than in aimless circles, to prevent unpleasant scratches which will show up even more when the piece is refinished. When sanding bare wood, use a good grade of paper (garnet paper); you will find that it cuts faster and finer and lasts longer than flint paper. After sanding, dampen the surface and let it dry; little whiskers of wood will stand up. Sand them off with a very fine sharp new paper, and repeat this operation until no more whiskers appear (two, three, or four times), and you will have a surface which will successfully take a smooth sealing coat. Any less effort is a waste of time.

Cleaning old furniture

Wash the surface with a cloth that has been wrung in a quart of hot water to which has been added ½ cup of turpentine and 2 tablespoons of boiled linseed oil; or in a quart of warm water to which has been added white soap flakes, and then a few tablespoons of turpentine. A good traditional combination cleaning and polishing solution for furniture is 1 cup each of boiled linseed oil, turpentine, and vinegar, plus 2 tablespoons of alcohol. Shake before using and rub on with a lint-free rag.

SUGGESTED READING

Albright, Alan B. "The Preservation of Water-logged Wood Specimens with Polyethylene Glycol." *Curator* 9:3 (1966): 228-34.

The use of P.E.G. 4000 and Ethanol.

Barkman, L. *The Preservation of the Wasa.* Stockholm: State Marine History Museum, 1965.

A general description of the treatment, materials, and equipment of the Swedish wooden warship.

"The Care of Wood Panels." *Museum* 8 (UNESCO, 1955): 139-64.

The whole issue is devoted to a technical discussion of wood, its properties, uses in relation to paintings, and treatment of various maladies.

Cartwright, Kenneth T., and Findlay, Walter P. *Decay of Timber and Its Prevention.* Brooklyn, N.Y.: Chemical Publishing Company, 1950.

Deschiens and Coste. "Protection of Works of Art in Carved Wood from the Attacks of Wood-eating Insects." *Museum* 10:1 (UNESCO. 1957).

Hunt, G. M. "Wood and Wood Products." *In Deterioration of Materials: Causes and Preventive Techniques.* Edited by Glenn A. Greathouse and Carl J. Wessel. New York: Reinhold Publishing Corporation, National Research Council, 1954.

Marsh, Moreton. *The Easy Expert in Collecting and Restoring American Antiques.* Philadelphia: J. B. Lippincott Company, 1959.

Moncrieff, A. "Review of Recent Literature on Wood." *Studies in Conservation* 13 (November, 1968).

A bibliography from 1960-1968 on the nature and care of wood.

Packard, Elizabeth C. "The Preservation of Polychromed Wood Sculpture by the Wax Immersion and Other Methods." *Museum News* 46 (October, 1967), Technical Supplement #19.

Plenderleith, Harold J. "Wood." In *The Conservation of Antiquities and Works of Art.* New York: Oxford University Press, 1956.

Rosenquist, Anna. "The Stabilizing of Wood Found in the Viking Ship of Oseberg." *Studies in Conservation* 4:1 (1959).

Published in London by the International Institute for the Conservation of Museum Objects. Techniques in the conservation of wood; methods which have and have not worked over a long period of time. (The publications of the I.I.C. have constant reference to the subject. It would be worthwhile to subscribe.)

Seborg, Ray M., and Inverarity, Robert B. "The Conservation of 200-year-old Water-logged Boats with Polyethylene Glycol." *Studies in Conservation* 7:4 (1962).

United States Department of Agriculture. *Wood Decay in Houses and How to Prevent and Control It.* Home and Garden Bulletin #73. Washington, D.C.: Government Printing Office, 1960.

_____, Forest Products Laboratory. *Wood Handbook* #72. Washington, D.C.: Government Printing Office, 1955.

_____, Forest Service. *Wood—Color and Kinds.* Agricultural Handbook #101. Washington, D.C.: Government Printing Office, 1956.

SUPPLIES

Preservatives (against dry rot and insects)
Creosote, hardware stores and lumber yards
"Decays-Not," Coopers Creek Chemical Corp., West Conshohocken, Penn.
"Penta," "Pentide," or other trade names may also be available in your locality; check with a local building contractor.
"Xylamon-BN-Clear," Desowag-Chemie GMBH, Bismarckstrasse 83-85, Düsseldorf, West Germany. Available in U.S. through Process Materials Corp., 329 Veterans Blvd., Carlstadt, N.J. 07072

Consolidating materials
'Git-Rot," 2-part resin, Aladdin Products, 18 Edgewood Place, Huntington Station, Long Island, N.Y. 11746
"Xylamon-LX-Hardening," Desowag-Chemie GMBH, Bismarckstrasse 83-85, Düsseldorf, West Germany. Recently became available in U.S. through Process Materials Corp., 329 Veterans Blvd., Carlstadt, N.J. 07072

Microcrystalline waxes
"Micro-Wax," Quaker State Oil Refining Corp., Bradford, Penn.
"Multi-Wax," Petroleum Specialities, Inc., 205 East 42nd St., New York, N.Y.
"Be-Square," and other grades, Petrolite Corp., Bareco Div., Ardmore, Penn.

Beeswax (available from most druggist and chemical supply houses).

Water-soluble polyethylene glycol waxes: used for consolidating weak water-logged wood, in a variety of molecular weights.

"Carbo-Wax," Union Carbide Company, 270 Park Ave., New York, N.Y. 10017

Other brands sold by Shell Oil (nationwide) and Dow Chemical Company, Midland, Mich.

10
Leather

THE NATURE OF SKIN

Skin, even more than any other organic material, is so adversely affected by excesses of heat, moisture, and/or micro-organisms that there is frequently nothing left of its original nature and characteristics; and even the best conservator or protein chemist may be unable to solve the problem.

Skin is composed of (a) the cuticle or epidermis; (b) the soft grain layer, containing the pigment, sweat glands, and hair follicles; and (c) the corium or basic skin, containing the fiber bundles. In life the skin, because it is composed of almost 60 percent water, is flexible, and the fiber bundles overlap and slide. After the death of the animal, when the flayed skin has dried out, it becomes stiff and inflexible.

The first step in processing a flayed skin, no matter how it will be subsequently used, is to scrape off all fat and flesh. If the fat is left on, the skin will rapidly deteriorate or become "fatburned" and full of weak spots. If any flesh is left on, it forms a perfect culture medium for all sorts of micro-organisms; and in the presence of moisture, the skin is soon reduced to a putrefied, stinking mess. The flesh and fat are usually removed by a combination of scraping with a blunt iron knife plus rubbing with absorbents like heated corn meal, bran, sawdust, or various earths.

A great variety of processing methods might then be applied to the skin. The cultural group that produced the artifact, the period of time from which it dates, and the use of the processed skin are all considerations in determining which of several methods might have been used on the piece. In order to understand how to treat artifacts made from animal skins, and to know what the limitations of treatment are, it is first necessary to know something about the traditional ways of preparing skins for use. The importance of this is to help a curator distinguish, for example, a tawed skin from a buckskin—and thus avoid the wrong treatment. A "regenerative" process applicable to a Siberian shaman's bag might be disastrous if applied to parchment. Thus, proper artifact identification is especially crucial to the care of leather goods. The reader is referred to the bibliographic sources listed with this chapter for an essential working knowledge of leather processing.

PRIMARY CARE OF SKIN AND LEATHER GOODS

Since leather objects which have been hardened by excess heat, powdered by acidic industrial fumes or degraded by moisture-loving bacteria cannot be brought back to life, the most important element in conserving leather is primary care. For longer life of your collections observe these specific practices:

1. Give the objects adequate ventilation and proper humidity. A relative humidity level of 50 to 60% is considered ideal. Below this level leather tends to dry out; and at much over 60% R.H., mildew and other unattractive bacteria go to work staining, eroding, and eventually eating up the leather.

2. Avoid extreme heat. Heat not only dries out the leather but may harden or permanently embrittle it. Keep your objects away from radiators and heat pipes.

3. Especially avoid the disastrous combination of heat and excessive moisture. A continuous drip from a leaky steam pipe will not only cockle parchment and harden leather, but will turn rawhide objects into hide glue. Once done you cannot reverse this process by any miracle salve.

4. Keep leather goods away from water. Soaked leather goods may shrink, cockle, and/or lose their shape or flexibility, depending on their original processing. Furs may lose their hair, and putrefactive organisms will have a chance to go to work. But any drying should be gradual and not accompanied by heat, lest the problem be compounded.

5. Avoid industrial fumes and sulphurous-, coke-, and coal-gas which can combine with minute particles of iron in leather to form a destructive acid, the action of which results in a nonreversible powdering of the leather. It may be necessary to resort to tightly sealed cases to minimize the trouble or, in the case of libraries containing a large number of leather bindings, to install air conditioning.

Knowing how skins are processed is essential to knowing the proper treatments for leather products.

6. Protect objects from moths, beetles, rats, and mice. Remember that many of these items represent potentially nutritious protein; and a mouse is just as happy to chew on Admiral Peary's mukluk or the cover of the Gutenberg Bible as on one of Pancho Villa's pistol belts.

Clean, tight storage areas plus spraying with a standard insecticide (such as Black Flag, Larvex, or Flit) will minimize the threat of insect damage. Paradiclorobenzene crystals (moth flakes) may also be used if the storage container is tight enough to exclude moths and other insects and if the temperature in the container is warm enough (90 degrees) that the flakes gradually evaporate to form a fumigating gas. (If you open the container after a few months and the flakes are still in solid form, the flakes are not doing any good.) The flakes must be in a strong enough concentration to be noticeable and somewhat irritating to human sensibilities in order to be effective. This applies to wool, leather, and furs.

CORRECTIVE MEASURES FOR LEATHER GOODS

While many conditions that affect leather goods are irreversible, there are some corrective measures that can be applied. Bear in mind, however, the necessity for proper identification of the type of leather and proceed with caution.

Stains and dirt

First brush off or vacuum as much of the dirt as possible. Then, in the case of leather goods, saddle soap can be applied with a lint-free rag and wiped off again. Lacking saddle soap, a thick solution can be made from a neutral soap, like Ivory flakes or Lux flakes (not detergent) and applied in the same manner as the saddle soap.

In the case of parchment or tawed skins, use *no* water. Sometimes using an art gum eraser or applying fuller's earth will modify the stain; but don't depend on it. Occasionally the use of a nonaqueous solvent like perchloroethylene mixed with an absorbent like fuller's earth or corn meal will lift a stain; but remember that in any product which has been treated with an oil or fat (like chamois or buckskin),

89

some of the fats may also be lifted out, leaving a stiff area.

Stains are particularly difficult to remove from tanned leather since the tannins accentuate the stain, particularly if it is iron-based, as are so many ink stains. While there are solvents which may remove them, the chances are more likely that they will degrade the leather or cause it to harden. In particular, one should avoid the use of detergents, especially the so-called "heavy duty" types. They may remove the spot but will also change the treated area into a hard, horny spot.

Furs should be treated by commercial furriers rather than with home remedies.

Mold and mildew

Mold and mildew are caused by too high humidity and lack of ventilation. Brush off as much as possible and expose the item to sunshine and fresh air for a few hours. If the item is of tanned leather it can be cleaned with saddle soap before sunning.

Leather and skin objects may be fumigated by placing them in a closed cabinet for twenty-four hours, together with a dish containing thymol crystals. The crystals are set in a dish over a heat source, like a sixty or seventy-five watt light bulb, close enough so the crystals will evaporate and create a fumigating gas. (If you notice a Listerine-like odor, the gas is being produced.) This treatment will kill the micro-organisms but will not offer lasting protection. A spray of 5% carbolic acid or oil of cloves in a water solution will offer a longer term treatment *but* only on leather goods that are not harmed by water. Wiping the leather with a wrung-out rag which has been dipped in a weak copper salt solution (like 3% copper sulphate in water) also tends to inhibit the growth of molds. The best long-term protection against mold and mildew is proper humidity and ventilation control.

Hard, hornlike leather

Some leathers have been processed in special ways, specifically to make them hard; and no softening greases can change them. Leather also may be unintentionally hardened by certain combinations of great heat and/or moisture or certain acids. Attempting to make it supple will only result in failure, and the possibility of cracking or breaking the article.

If the article is already broken, it can be consolidated just as one mends wood or ceramics. An adhesive like Elmer's white glue or Duco cement will hold thick pieces, but if the fragments are thin, the object may need to be backed with linen canvas or attached to a flat surface, such as particle board, with the above-mentioned adhesives.

Objects which have been consolidated may have a follow-up treatment of wax polish or synthetic lacquer if desired; but it is understood that this is a cosmetic treatment, and not a restorative.

Needless to say, such procedures are for objects which have been permanently hardened through age or accident. Rawhide trunks and parchment are naturally stiff and do not need softening.

Powdery leather

Leather that has been permanently damaged, usually by an acidic atmosphere, may become powdery. Frequently oils, wax dressings, and the like are added, but they are of *no* avail except to "cheer up" the looks of the item temporarily. The only real consolidant is the use of polyvinylacetate emulsion or synthetic resin. But these will alter the looks of the object and make it stiff permanently. Be certain that the need is important enough to warrant this treatment. A 10% potassium lactate solution is currently recommended as a buffering solution to protect new leather against powdery deterioration and is being used by many libraries. But keep in mind that this treatment is of *no* avail for books which are already powdery.

Wet leather

Leather which has come out of sunken ships, wells, or archaeological sites and has been continuously wet needs special handling.

First of all, do not let it dry out lest it shrivel to a tiny shrunken mass. Put it in a jar of water with about half a teaspoon of carbolic acid per quart of water to inhibit the growth of bacteria.

There are a number of treatments for drying out organic materials using baths of alcohol and ether plus vacuum; but they are expensive and potentially quite dangerous. They should be left alone by the novice. Other methods involve soaking or rubbing the object in sulphonated neat's-foot or castor oil, vaseline, or other mixtures. Sometimes they seem to work; but results have not been consistent to date. One water-soluble synthetic wax (polyethylene glycol 1500), however, seems to have had much better results than the others. The object is soaked in the melted wax for a few days until the water is extracted from the leather and replaced by wax.

If treatments seem too drawn out or complex, then keep the object immersed in an antiseptic water solution until you can have something done about it.

Dry or stiff normal leather

It may be assumed that during their useful life many objects in a collection, like boots, saddlebags, baggage, cartridge holders, belts, and harnesses have been subjected to normal wear and tear, exposure to heat, alternate wetting and drying, and the like. Many of these items may be in basically sound condition, needing only lubrication and suppling to make them acceptable for exhibition. Let me emphasize that lubrication refers to treatment of furs, tawed, curried, pickled, and tanned leather, but *not* to parchment, vellum, or rawhide objects.

The type of lubrication and the amount of suppling will depend on the class of object. Experts tend to be in disagreement as to which oils, waxes, and greases are most effective for some objects. Some workers in the field consider saddle soap insufficient in lubricating properties; others consider neat's-foot and castor oils as much too messy. Don't feel too badly if your reading turns up conflicting advice; leather chemistry is still a field with many unknowns, and there is quite some room for practical long-term observation. So be aware of the fact that while some of the following hints may represent the consensus of general opinion in this field, some of them reflect the author's own opinions.

Harnesses

Generally work harness and traces have been traditionally treated

Do not try to soften leather products that were purposely made stiff and hard, such as this fire bucket.

with neat's-foot oil and this treatment may be continued. It is, however, rather messy. After being oiled and allowed to stand over-night, the harness should be wiped with a dry cloth to remove the excess. The harness should then be stored or exhibited in such a way that it does not stain walls or surrounding objects.

Russet (light brown) harness was used by the more affluent for city driving or Sunday rides, and should be kept as close to its original color as possible. Avoid heavy oils like castor oil or neat's-foot oil and use an emulsion dressing or saddle soap. A tan or neutral shoe cream may also be used for dressing and polishing.

Shoes and Boots

Dress shoes and boots should be treated normally with saddle soap, using a rather wet, foamy mixture to ensure that it penetrates the leather. If the boots were originally meant to be soft they can be carefully manipulated while still damp, while at the same time rubbing in the mixture. When dry, they may be buffed with a cloth or soft brush.

Old work or farm boots will often be stiffer and show more signs of neglect than dress boots and usually require more effort to soften. They may be cleansed of dirt and/or mildew with a washing of either Lux or Ivory flakes or saddle soap; however, to attempt polishing these items would be meretricious. If the boots are still stiff after being treated with saddle soap, a second stage will be necessary. Dampen the leather and follow with one or more applications of an emulsion dressing. (If you don't wish to make up your own, a commercial one, "Lexol," is satisfactory.) As you rub in the dressing, keep flexing the leather until it reaches the desired softness. The boots or shoes should then be tightly stuffed with newspaper overnight in order to minimize any wrinkles or turnup at the toes.

An alternative to emulsion dressing is a mixture of four parts of neat's-foot oil and one part pine tar, melted together with enough beeswax (one to two parts) to make a stiff paste when the mixture is cool. The addition of pine tar tends to inhibit mold growth; and the beeswax keeps the neat's-foot oil from being quite so messy.

The boots are dampened and allowed to stand for a few minutes before the dressing is applied. Although one thinks of oil and water as being incompatible, it has been my experience that slightly damp leather seems to take dressings better than bone-dry boots. (Whether the dressing "follows" the dampness as it leaves the leather or not I do not know—I have no scientific explanation.) The oil-wax-tar dressing is applied to the boot with the hand; the heat of the hand, plus friction, facilitates penetration. Keep one hand inside the boot and flex as you rub the dressing with the other hand until the boots are soft enough. Stuff with paper overnight and rub with a piece of toweling next day to remove any excess.

Military Accoutrements

Cartridge boxes, shot flasks, military accoutrements, and saddle bags or dispatch boxes are usually made of rather heavy leather, are normally somewhat stiff, and thus need only a cleaning with saddle soap. This may be followed by an appropriate color of shoe polish if there are nicks or scars. Any of these items which are hinged, such as dispatch cases or cartridge pouches, should receive a treatment of dressing on the flesh (or inner side) to prevent them from cracking. If they are already broken off, the only solution is to make an inner reinforcement of thin leather or heavy canvas; and, depending on the original construction or aesthetics of the object, the reinforcing piece may be stitched or glued on with white glue. If it is to be glued, be certain that the leather has not been greased or oiled or the glue will not stick. Appropriate dressings for the hinged areas would be "Lexol," British Museum Leather Dressing, a 50/50 anhydrous lanolin and neat's-foot oil, or one of the new silicone leather dressings.

Fur Skins

Since most traditional methods of dressing fur involved the use of emulsions, the same methods may be used for most ethnological specimens. The skin should be slightly dampened on the flesh side with a wet sponge, and allowed to set for about ten minutes to relax it. Then follow with an emulsion dressing. If you have a fur coat that is a product of modern civilization, you should perhaps

94

farm it out to a furrier. For one thing, such coats usually have a lining; and they also are made of skins of small beasts and are consequently much more fragile than fur garments worn by Indians, Eskimos, or Lapps. Don't be disappointed if there is some hair loss from ethnological specimens. The original methods of processing by many native groups make this almost inevitable.

Bookbindings

It is not possible to list here all of the many combinations which can be used for dressings. For additional information you are referred to the reading list, especially to the publication by Carolyn Horton. But a few general remarks are in order.

Gold leaf lettering or ornamentation is frequently found on old bindings and may be susceptible to moisture. If you use saddle soap or emulsion dressings on the binding, *go easy* and use as little water as possible, lest you lift the leaf.

If you use any of the oil or oil-wax mixtures, use as little as possible, and rub in with your hands to facilitate penetration. When you are rubbing it in, put a sheet of wax paper between the binding and the flyleaf to prevent grease stains on the paper. After you have finished dressing the bindings, stand the book on end overnight (if it is strong enough) with the book spread open a bit. Then rub off any excess to prevent staining. If you are going to use potassium lactate buffering solution on the leather, do it before you put on any dressing.

There are some problems in leather as in wood and all organic materials which are insoluble because deterioration has already gone too far. Therefore it bears reemphasis that the conservation of *all* organic materials takes place basically through proper care and storage, rather than in the conservation laboratory. Long life for the objects is the concern of the director, curator, and registrar.

SUGGESTED READING

"Alaska Sealskins," in *CIBA Review*, No. 94 (October, 1952).

Banks, P. N. "Treating Leather Bookbindings" (xeroxed), Newberry Library, Chicago.

"Cleaning Buckskin," in *Clearing House for (South) Western Museum News Letter*, No. 192 (February, 1956).

"Cleaning Deer and Other Skin," *ibid.*, No. 89 (July, 1947).

"Early History of Tanning," in *CIBA Review*, No. 81 (August, 1950).

Ewers, J. C. *Blackfeet Crafts*. Lawrence, Kansas: Haskell Institute, 1945.

Guldbeck, Per E. "Leather: Its Understanding and Care." *History News* 24 (April, 1969), Technical Leaflet #1 rev. ed.

"Fur," in *CIBA Review*, No. 114 (April, 1956).

Horton, Carolyn. *Cleaning and Preserving Bindings and Related Materials*. Library Technology Program. Chicago: American Library Association, 1967.

Kephart, Horace. *Camping and Woodcraft*. New York: Macmillan Company, 1944. (Part II, pages 298-326.)

The Leather Worker in 18th Century Williamsburg. Williamsburg Craft Series. Williamsburg, Virginia: Colonial Williamsburg, Inc., 1967.

Lollar, R. M. "Leather," in *Deterioration of Materials*. Edited by Glenn A. Greathouse and C. J. Wessel. New York: Reinhold, 1954.

"Micro-organic Attack On Textiles and Leather," in *CIBA Review*, No. 100 (October, 1953).

Plenderleith, H. J. "Animal Skin and Skin Products, . . . Parchment," in *The Conservation of Antiquities and Works of Art*. New York: Oxford University Press, 1956.

"The Problem of Softening Stiffened Leather," in *Clearing House for (South) Western Museums News Letter*, No. 97 (March, 1948).

Rogers, J. S., and C. W. Beebe. *Leather Bookbindings, How to Preserve Them*. Leaflet No. 398. Washington, D.C.: U.S. Department of Agriculture, 1956.

"Tanning in Modern Times," in *CIBA Review*, No. 118 (January, 1957).

Todd, William. "Conservation of Skin and Leather" (mimeographed), History Branch, Department of Travel and Publicity, Toronto, Ontario.

Velich, R. "The Repair and Cleaning of an Old Painted Buffalo Robe," in *Curator*, VIII (May, 1965).

Waterer, John W. "Leather," in *A History of Technology*. Vol. II. New York: Oxford University Press, 1956.

Werner, A. E. "Consolidation of Fragile Objects," in *Recent Advances in Conservation*. Ed. G. Thompson. London: Butterworths, 1963.

Welsh, Peter C. *Tanning in the United States to 1850.* United States National Museum Bulletin 242. Washington, D.C.: Government Printing Office, 1964.

SUPPLIES

Deacidifier and buffering salt—for protecting leather bindings against decay.
Leather Dressing (New York Public Library formula).
 TALAS—Technical Library Service, 104 Fifth Ave., New York, N.Y. 10011
British Museum Leather Dressing
 Fisher Scientific Co. (offices nationwide). Main office: 52 Fadem Road, Springfield, New Jersey 07081
Linen for backing of permanently stiffened or broken pieces of horny leather.
 Utrecht Linens, Inc., 33 Thirty-Fifth Street, Brooklyn, New York
Polyethylene glycols
 Union Carbide Co., 270 Park Avenue, New York, N.Y. 10017
 (Also sold by the Shell Oil Company and Dow Chemical Company.)
"Lexol" emulsion for softening and flexing stiff but sound leather.
 The Lexol Corporation, West Caldwell, New Jersey.
 (Also hardware and shoe stores.)
Sulphonated castor oil (Turkey Red oil)
 Fisher Scientific Company
Sulphonated Neat's-foot Oil
 Most hardware stores
Phenol (carbolic acid) Poison! Easily absorbed through the skin!
 Pharmacists or drug stores.
"White glues" or plastic emulsion glues. (Elmer's, LePage's, etc.)
 Usually found at hardware stores or lumber yards.
Thymol crystals
 Chemical supply houses or some pharmacists.

11
Ferrous Objects

PROBLEMS IN MAINTAINING FERROUS OBJECTS

Rusting (Oxidation) is the number one enemy, especially when augmented by chloride salts, which are found in common salt, road salts, sea water, and sea air. *Overtreatment* is the number two enemy. Although iron in contact with water, acids, or chlorides will corrode quickly, normally corrosion proceeds slowly. Leave the object alone unless you know what you are doing, and unless you are certain that you want to remove the surface layer.

Think first: was the original surface shiny or not? While a look of dusty decay and neglect is to be deplored in a museum, it is even more appalling to a collector or conservator to see displays of work tools, utensils, and firearms that have been ground and polished to a bright metal finish which they never had during their useful life. Many gunlocks and barrels, for instance, were given a blue, brown, or case-hardened finish during their manufacture, and removal of any or all of these thin layers lessens their museum (and market) value. Many forge-made tools still retain their dark carbide scale, the result of prolonged heating in a charcoal fire. This is part of the documentation of the object and often helps to distinguish an early piece from a modern reproduction that is darkened with flat black paint. Aside from their aesthetic or documentary value, these dark patinas also form a stable protective coating, unlike the active corrosion represented by yellow, red, or brown rust.

PRIMARY PROTECTION OF FERROUS OBJECTS

Ferrous objects in good condition should be safeguarded from high humidity, marine air, chloride salts, industrial vapors, acid conditions, and fingerprints. If a clean environment with low humidity cannot be provided, then some type of protective coating should be used. Before any coating is applied, be certain that the object is dry, and free of dirt, rust, and grease.

Clear hard coats

Boiled linseed oil or oil-resin varnishes have long been used as a waterproofing; but it has been gradually discovered that moisture can penetrate, and that the protection was more apparent than real. At present there are a number of dips and sprays formulated from synthetic resins which give better protection. But even these are effective only if the coating is unbroken and if no moisture and salts are trapped beneath the surface. These coatings are usually rather shiny, which may give a meretricious appearance to some objects.

Wax coats

These offer less mechanical protection than synthetic resins; but, on the other hand, they have no objectionable shine. One can use traditional waxes like candelilla, carnauba, and beeswax, or micro-crystalline waxes that are available in white or amber and in a variety of melting ranges. When built up in layers, some waxes lose their transparency and on pitted iron or rough castings cause an unnatural appearance. Test the wax before applying it to a large surface.

Heavy oils and greases

These are useful for objects that are to be stored for long periods or under adverse climate conditions. They are generally too messy for practical use in a small museum with limited collections.

Silicone spray

A combination invisible protective coat and lubricant used in hospitals is a silicone spray called "Sil-Spray." Being a spray, it can get into threads, interstices, and generally hard-to-reach areas. It clings tightly, resists handling and high temperatures, and does not change the appearance of the object. The vehicle, which feels like a grade of mineral spirits, can be rubbed off easily with a cloth, and the silicone remains behind in the pores of the metal.

Clear coating

A clear, matte coating that gives good protection to smooth or pitted surfaces is "SP220." The liquid is diluted with water, the

A mid-18th century British gun lock, cleaned by the slow but effective method of polishing with fine silicon carbide paper. It reveals engraving and stamp marks and creates a smooth polished surface that keeps out moisture.

objects are dipped and allowed to dry. The resulting film is thin, invisible, and nonsticky. Although it is not recommended by the manufacturers for outdoor use, I have found nonetheless that test pieces stood up well to six months outside exposure.

Heavy duty coatings and paints

While usually too thick or otherwise aesthetically objectionable on small items, these are the only answer for gross objects such as cast-iron cannons, grill work, chains, anchors, and rough castings or forged objects that will be subjected to environmental extremes. Some brands are said to be successfully applied over rusted or damp metal. But it must be emphasized that for best results the metal should be dry, free from scale, loose rust, and chloride salts.

Calcium plumbate and the traditional red lead, available at all hardware stores, are two effective metal primers. However, since they are both rather soft even after drying, it is usually desirable to have a finishing coat based on a harder iron oxide-pigmented paint. Zinc chromate is another good primer available in various formulations from most hardware stores. Tough epoxy-resin paints formulated for boating use are available at most marine supply houses, although inlanders may have difficulty locating them. These epoxy paints must be mixed and applied carefully, so be sure to read the directions before using them.

If your museum is concerned with old carriages, farm machinery, wagons, and steam power takeoffs, most of which were painted a variety of colors on the body or running gear, consider "Derusto" or "Rustoleum" (available at hardware stores). These paints are relatively inexpensive and come in a variety of colors. But do not purchase them in a spray-can form if you can avoid it. Not only are they more expensive this way, but the rather heavy oils and pigments are forever becoming clogged, no matter how careful you are about shaking the can and keeping the nozzle clean.

A black coating for marine use is "Rust Preventative 150" (available from Service Industries) which is said to be quite resistant to salt penetration. Its melting range (120-130°F), however, would prohibit its use on such equipment as stoves or steam boilers that are used

Before   *After*

in live demonstrations.

Tannate coatings: An old trapper's trick which has been redis-
covered by the scientific world (see the articles by J. B. Pelikan)
is to boil or scrub lightly rusted objects in a solution of water and
tannic acid. This forms a stable coating of iron tannate. The
proportions and boiling time are empirical rather than specific.

CLEANING RUSTED IRON

Removing light rust

Light rust may be removed by rubbing with 000 (or 0000 if
available) steel wool and kerosene, which will remove rust but not
bluing. The kerosene must then be removed with white gas or acetone, since it picks up water and will cause further rusting. "Tri-M-ite"
400 abrasive and oil will clean and polish metal parts, but will also
remove any patina present. If this is no problem, persistent abrading
will give not only a smooth pleasing surface, but one that will have
fewer pockets for corrosion to take hold of again.

Boiling in vinegar

Boiling objects in vinegar will remove a surprising amount of rust.
Take the objects out of the solution occasionally, and scrub with
000 steel wool or a bristle brush, to remove loosened rust and scum.
After cleaning, rinse the object thoroughly in hot water to which a
bit of washing soda has been added to neutralize the effect of the
acid—about a tablespoon of soda per quart of water. Then rinse
the object again in hot distilled water. Dry the object in a 225°F.
oven or under an infrared heat lamp. If any slight rust appears after
the object is dry, it may be polished off with 000 steel wool.

Strong acids

Solutions using strong acids (like sulphuric or nitric acids) are
often used as pickling agents to remove rust and scale, but unless they
are thoroughly rinsed off afterwards they will lead to renewed
rusting. Strong acids are also hazardous and tricky for the amateur;
their use is not generally advised.

Cleaning rusted iron, especially small pieces, by means of strong acid solutions results in loss of detail, eating away of thin sections, and deep pitting.

Commercial rust removers

Commercial rust removers are generally quite powerful in their action, and when heated or used in concentration can affect one's eyes, nose, and throat as do strong acids. In addition, when commercial rust removers are used, even in the recommended dilutions, one must periodically check the action of the solution on the object being treated. Otherwise there may be extensive etching and pitting of the surface; and in the case of thin objects, such as knife blades or sheet iron utensils, they may be reduced to a mass of particles in the bottom of the container. Many rust removers today leave a thin gray green protective film on the cleaned metal. If you find this color objectionable you may either paint over it with a coating of black or use a different method of cleaning.

Mechanical methods

Rust encrustation can also be removed a bit at a time (about 1/16″ squares) by picking away with a dental pick. Be sure to hold the pick at right angles to the work rather than at a slant in order to attain pressure and control. Used in this way it exerts tremendous force. But wear safety glasses when doing this; and be sure that there is coherent metal under the rust, or you may end up with a bench full of rust particles and no object. This is a definite possibility in materials from an archaeological site. Test the object with a magnet; if it is not attracted, it is rust all the way through. On no account try to knock off the rust with a hammer; and do not use a blow torch! A torch may pop off loose particles, but it may also cause other deposits to fuse and become chemically insoluble.

In cleaning rusty surfaces, do not use power grinding wheels or wire wheels. They may remove rust, but will leave noneradicable scars and will remove metal, damaging the piece permanently. Not only are scars and scratches from coarse files and grinders difficult to remove, but in doing so you are removing original material, blurring edges and inscriptions, and destroying what you intended to preserve.

102

TREATING COMPLETELY RUSTED OBJECTS

Rusted objects that do not respond to a magnet require special care to keep them intact. First soak the object in clean hot water for a few hours and then allow it to cool overnight in the water bath. This process is repeated each day for several days (with fresh changes of water) until the object is free from soluble salts that could otherwise cause expansion and popping off of pieces of rust.

To test whether or not the soluble chloride salts have been washed out, add a few drops each of silver nitrate solution and nitric acid to a test tube containing a sample of the rinse water. If there is still some chloride present, a silvery gray cloud will form in the water, and the rinsing process must be repeated. (Test with clean tap water first to be sure that the effect is not caused by chlorine in the local water supply. If this is so, use well water or distilled water for the final rinse). Then dry the object by heating it in a low oven (200°-250°F.) for an hour or more, depending on the size of the object. Next drop the object in a bath of molten wax until all bubbling ceases, lift it out, and remove excess wax. (Be certain to heat the wax in a water bath or double boiler if you are indoors. A gallon of wax boiling over on a gas stove could be disastrous. Keep a Class "B" fire extinguisher close by.) For large objects you may have to improvise a unit out of doors with a container made to order by a local tinsmith, or with commercial tubs or stock-watering tanks. Heating the mixture may require electrical resistance heaters, a gas fire, or steam coils. Besides taking precautions against fire, be wary of the explosion potential. When wood or porous metal objects are dipped in molten wax, there is frequently a certain percentage of water driven off, which, being heavier than the wax, settles to the bottom of the pot or tank. When the wax has cooled and hardened and is being heated for the next use, the thin layer of water underneath heats first. It can build up dangerous steam pressure if it is trapped under the solid block of wax. Either the wax should be drained off after each use, or there should be a petcock at the lowest part of the tank to drain off the water, or the

heating elements should be set into the sides rather than the bottom of the tank.

Rusted marine objects

When an object is brought up from an undersea site it is often difficult to discern, in the masses of mud, sand, coral, and corrosion, how much is still coherent metal. The extent of corrosion depends on a number of factors: the length of time the object has been submergèd, the temperature and salinity of the water, the degree to which the object has become covered with mud or marine growth, or the extent to which it has been in close association with other metals, resulting in electrochemical activity that protects one object at the expense of the other. Because of this range of factors the chemistry of conserving submerged iron objects is rather complex; and the answers for preserving a cannon dug up from a freshwater lake will not necessarily work for one taken from the Bay of Fundy or the Florida Keys. Articles by Plenderleith, Gettens, H. Peterson, Evans, and M. Peterson (in the suggested readings) should be studied before you attempt to clean corroded marine artifacts. Such objects pose more problems than dry land artifacts because of their chloride content, and because there is a greater danger of destroying evidence and outlines in attempting to remove calcareous growths and corrosion layers.

SUGGESTED READING

Evans, Ulick R. *The Corrosion and Oxidation of Metals: Scientific Principles and Practical Applications*. London: Edward Arnold Ltd., 1961.

Gettens, Rutherford J. "Mineral Alteration Products on Ancient Metal Objects." In *Recent Advances in Conservation*. London: Butterworths, 1963.

Greathouse, Glenn A., and Wessel, Carl J., eds. *Deterioration of Materials: Causes and Preventive Techniques*. New York: Reinhold Publishing Corporation, National Research Council, 1954.

Organ, R. M. "The Consolidation of Fragile Metallic Objects." In *Recent*

Advances in Conservation. London: Butterworths, 1963.

Pelikan, J. B. "The Use of Polyphosphate Complexes in the Conservation of Iron and Steel Objects." *Studies in Conservation* 9 (May, 1964).

_____. "Conservation of Iron with Tannin." *Studies in Conservation* 11 (August, 1966).

Peterson, Harold L. "The Care of Antique Firearms." In *NRA Gun Collectors Handbook.* Washington, D.C.: National Rifle Association of America, 1959.

_____. "The Conservation of Metals." *History News* 23 (February, 1968), Technical Leaflet #10, rev. ed.

Peterson, Mendel. *History Under the Sea: A Manual for Underwater Exploration.* Rev. ed. Washington, D.C.: Smithsonian Institution Press, 1965.

Plenderleith, Harold J. *The Conservation of Antiquities and Works of Art: Treatment, Repair, and Restoration.* New York: Oxford University Press, 1956.

Plenderleith, Harold J., and Toracca, G. "The Conservation of Metals in the Tropics." In *The Conservation of Cultural Property.* Paris: UNESCO, 1968.

Wheeler, Ardis H., and Holmquist, June D., eds. *Diving Into the Past: Theories, Techniques and Application of Underwater Archaeology.* St. Paul, Minn.: Minnesota Historical Society, Conference on Underwater Archaeology, 1964.

SUPPLIES

Silicone Spray

"Sil-Spray," Duxe Products, Cincinnati, Ohio

Coatings

"SP220" Service Industries, 2103 East Somerset, Philadelphia, Penn.

"Rust Preventative 150," Service Industries, 2103 East Somerset, Philadelphia, Penn.

12
Copper and Copper Alloys

Copper and its alloys—gun metal, bronze, bell metal, and brass—are all relatively stable materials; and although the archaeologist and marine salvager will encounter corrosion products, these metals normally present few problems to the historical society conservator.

CLEANING CUPROUS OBJECTS

Before the museum conservator uncorks his brass polish, he should know about the finish or patina of the object to be treated. Some nineteenth-century bronzes were darkened with chemicals at the time they were made, in order to give them the antique look that was popular then and still is today to some extent. Some brass cavalry bugles and military candle lanterns were made with a dark finish and a matte, almost pitted-look surface that would not reflect sunlight. Scientific and navigation instruments were often given a clear varnish or a dark bituminous "japanned" finish to protect them against weathering. And, of course, certain classes of artifacts and art objects have acquired stable patina which is generally considered aesthetically desirable. This may include such diversified items as eighteenth-century cannon, Chinese Buddhas, or Etruscan bowls. It can be argued that when such objects were new they were meant to look shiny; but since connoisseurs consider the patina important, one should be aware of this body of opinion.

These remarks are by way of warning, as with iron and steel, not to be hasty in deciding to clean an object down to bare metal. Original surfaces and subsequent chemical alterations which are' of interest to the research historian and the scientist may be lost forever.

Simple oxidation

Characterized by a dull reddish or brown film, this condition usually responds to commercial brass polishes like "Porters Friend" or "Brasso" which contain fine whiting in an ammonia solution. Such a polish can be made by combining: ½ part aqua ammonia, 1 part denatured alcohol, 1 part distilled water, and enough fine gilders' whiting to make a thin paste. (Fine whiting can be purchased from an art supply store, if not available from a paint store.) Be careful of your nose when pouring the aqua ammonia—it is potent! You may prefer to have a druggist mix it for you. The proportions for this polish are not critical; a bit less water can be used if desired.

Warning: Beware of some of the paste cleaners sold on the market as copper brighteners, as some of them are markedly acidic or contain chlorides. Avoid the use of abrasive papers or steel wool because they are far too abrasive on nonferrous metals. Avoid, too, the old cliché of salt and lemon juice (or vinegar) as a cleaner, as the chlorides in the salt will simply complicate future cleaning.

Heavy oxidation

If polish will not remove the dull film, stripping solutions may be employed. A 5% solution of citric acid (1 ounce per pint of water) will clean off either dull film or corrosion. Pick the item out of the solution occasionally and scrub it with a fiber brush, or rub it with a dampened rag to which has been applied a dab of whiting or rottenstone. This will speed up the action; and in this way you can also check to be certain that the metal is not being "scalded" or over-cleaned. After removal from the bath, rinse the object in water to which about 5% of washing soda has been added. This will neutralize any remaining acid. Then rinse in clear water and dry.

Do not immerse an object in the above mentioned cleaning solution if the object is made of *two* or more diverse metals. There is a good possibility of setting up electrochemical reactions between the metals, with consequent undesirable side effects. For the same reason plated goods should not be immersed in this solution lest the plating be stripped off.

If corrosion is so extensive that there is doubt as to whether there is coherent metal underneath, do not attempt to clean the object, but leave it for an expert.

CONFRONTING SPECIAL PROBLEMS

Chloride salts

Copper-based items that have been under the sea or in certain soils and have acquired chloride salts have a tendency to pick up moisture from the air. Unless the object is kept quite dry, or is treated by electrolysis or specialized chemical processes it will break down. These treatments, however, may also result in the removal of stable or desirable patina if incorrectly done and are therefore not recommended for the novice.

One method that is generally considered safe for the novice, and that will not destroy patina, is the use of sodium sesquicarbonate. Make a 5% solution of sodium sesquicarbonate (1 ounce per pint of distilled water) and allow the object to soak in it for several weeks. Then rinse the object in fresh water and test for chlorides (see page 103). If necessary, make a fresh solution of sodium sesquicarbonate and soak again until the final rinse water tests clear. As with the citric acid method do not soak an object made of two dissimilar metals.

Calcareous (limy) deposits

These deposits may be found in both excavations and underwater sites. While acids are sometimes used to dissolve them, a 10% solution (1½ ounces per pint of water) of sodium hexametaphosphate ("Calgon") in water will soften the crust with less danger of destroying the patina. If you heat the solution or let the object soak longer than necessary to soften the crusts, you might lose some of the patina as well. Check your work periodically.

APPLYING PROTECTIVE FINISHES

Wax polishes give relatively slight mechanical protection but are easy to remove with petroleum solvents like mineral spirits. Lacquer is harder and lasts longer. But it does change the luster of the piece; and, of course, once it is scratched, the oxidation starts all over again, and the old lacquer must be removed to repolish the piece. Theoretically lacquer thinner should do the job, but in practice it often takes vast amounts to actually remove the lacquer rather than just thinning it down. In addition, lacquer thinner is toxic and highly flammable. A mixture that will break down the lacquer film is a 50/50 solution of aqua ammonia and denatured alcohol. This mixture is extremely irritating to the senses. The object, covered with a rag wetted in this mixture, should be left in a closed chamber or bell jar. Because the fumes are so toxic and irritating, this is a last resort remedy. Consider the hazards of the local environment before deciding whether or not to lacquer.

SUGGESTED READING

Jedrzejewska, H. "The Conservation of Ancient Bronzes." *Studies in Conservation* 9 (February, 1964).

_____. "Some New Experiments in the Conservation of Ancient Bronzes." In *Recent Advances in Conservation*. London: Butterworths, 1963.

Kauffman, Henry J. *American Copper and Brass*. Camden, N.J.: Thomas Nelson and Sons, 1968.
Artifacts made in America, their styles and variations from some European and modern ware, plus something about the technology of the brazier and coppersmith.

Organ, R. M. "Aspects of Bronze Patina and Its Treatment." *Studies in Conservation* 8 (February, 1963).

_____. "The Examination and Treatment of Bronze Antiquities." In *Recent Advances in Conservation*. London: Butterworths, 1963.

13
Tin, Pewter, and Lead

TIN

While tin can be corroded by prolonged exposure to combinations of air and moisture and some acids, it is, on the whole, quite stable. For example, bars of tin that were taken up after being 100 years in the holds of sunken Confederate raiders off the coast of North Carolina were for the most part relatively uncorroded. The layman thinks of tin as being an ephemeral, easily rusted material because of his association of tin with the term "tin cans." Tin cans and tinware are basically sheet-iron protected by only a microscopically thin layer of tin, and it is the iron that corrodes after the thin tin layer has been worn or scratched away. Because of its rarity and price, a relatively heavy inner coating of tin is used only on better grade copper and brass cooking wares.

While tin is stable it is also soft, and a curator wishing to brighten tin wares or tin objects should use only the finest polishes. On no account use acids or alkalis which are capable of stripping off or destroying the tin.

PEWTER

Contemporary pewter (Britannia metal) is basically tin to which small percentages of antimony and copper have been added to give hardness and sharper impressions in casting. While traditional pewter was also based on tin plus antimony, it often contained a greater or lesser amount of lead. The percentage of lead depended upon: (a) the availability of tin (always more expensive and rarer than lead); (b) the integrity of the craftsman, since it is difficult for the layman to detect the percentage of lead inclusion; and (c) the ultimate use of the object fabricated. For example, large amounts of lead would be dangerous in food and drink containers but would be harmless and acceptable in candlesticks and organ pipes. Thus, depending on the lead/tin ratio in a traditional piece of pewter, the environment in which it was kept, and the uses to which it was put, one's collection may include a range from pieces that have a pleasant patina to those that are pitted wrecks.

Dull pewter may be polished by fine abrasives like rottenstone or gilders' whiting mixed in a carrier like oil or alcohol. If the metal does not respond to this treatment, do not try harsh abrasives or steel wool, since pewter is even softer than any of the cuprous (copper-based) alloys.

Although there are electrochemical reduction methods that will remove certain types of heavy corrosion, their use sometimes produces a clean surface at the expense of loss of smoothness, or blurred lines, inscriptions, and stampmarks, all of which are a loss both aesthetically and for research purposes. The acids or alkalis commercially used to clean pewter are inimical to the piece if their action is not thoroughly understood, and if the residues are not completely removed after washing. Do not be in a hurry to have this done, and have it done only by someone who thoroughly understands and can control the process. Occasionally pewter suffers from a form of physical alteration of its structure, known as "tin-pest," a powdery crystalline condition confused with corrosion. Tin-pest is thought to be the result of prolonged exposure to cold; but in any event nothing can be done to bring back pewter in this condition. Before attempting to clean heavily corroded pewter do read the articles listed in the suggested readings.

LEAD

While lead is as shiny as tin when freshly cast or cut, in a short time it acquires a characteristic stable dark grey patina. Lead is, however, quite sensitive to any acid vapors, or to acid and moisture. For this reason lead objects that have been in industrial atmospheres, handled by sweaty hands, or exhibited in old-fashioned oak wood cases (high in tannic acid) will soon acquire a powdery white surface, evidence of unstable lead carbonate.

The best course is prevention—keeping lead objects free from an acid environment. There are procedures for cleaning and stabilizing corroded lead; but all of the safe methods are somewhat complicated. If you have a number of lead pieces in bad condition it is recommended that you consult the bibliography first. (See especially the articles in Plenderleith's handbook and his article in the 1968 UNESCO publication.)

SUGGESTED READING

Caley, E. R. "Coatings and Incrustations on Lead Objects from the Agora and the Method Used for Their Removal." *Studies in Conservation* 2 (October, 1955).

Plenderleith, Harold J. *The Conservation of Antiquities and Works of Art: Treatment, Repair, and Restoration.* New York: Oxford University Press, 1956.

_____. "The Decay and Conservation of Museum Objects of Tin." *Studies in Conservation* 1 (June, 1953).

_____, and Toracca G. "The Conservation of Metals in the Tropics." In *The Conservation of Cultural Property.* Paris: UNESCO, 1968.

14
Gold, Silver, and Ambiguous Silvery-looking Materials

GOLD

Gold is a stable material without corrosion problems. But when cleaning other metals in association with gold, avoid harsh abrasives lest the gold be scratched.

SILVER

In a museum setting it is most important to provide an environment that will not cause tarnishing of silver. Even though silver is considered one of the "noble" metals, it is quite susceptible to tarnishing from minute amounts of sulphur compounds in the air, necessitating cleaning and polishing of the objects. Frequent polishing (even with the finest polishes) leads to loss of detail through the constant wearing away of this soft metal, and in the case of plated ware eventually results in exposure of the base metal.

Most housewives are unhappily aware of the results when silver comes in contact with the sulphur contained in rubber goods, eggs, coal gas, and industrial environments. But it is less well known that household synthetic detergents frequently contain sulphur, plus phosphorous compounds, which cause particularly stubborn stains. Latex paints which are popular for exhibition work contain sulphur, and when used in a closed case with heat-producing incandescent lights (or the warm ballasts of fluorescent fixtures) can cause the tarnishing of silver in a few days.

Therefore, since silver is so soft and easily worn by excess polishing and handling, it behooves the museum conservator to provide a sympathetic environment that keeps tarnishing to a minimum.

Protecting

Keeping the silver away from sulphurous atmosphere and materials is obviously the best form of protection. One method is to store the silver in soft tissue paper, excluding outside air. But be sure to get a good grade of tissue that is suitable—check with your jeweler. The usual department store wrapping tissue made of ground wood pulp is not suitable. Putting the silver into airtight polyethylene bags will further help to prevent tarnish.

113

For exhibition use, the silver may be coated with Krylon or with lacquer spray, although these will slightly change the appearance of the silver. An alternative is to put anti-tarnish paper in inconspicuous or hidden areas of the case. An anti-tarnish cloth can also be made from silk that has been soaked in a lead acetate solution. (See Plenderleith, p. 215, for full directions.)

Cleaning

Polishes

You can make an inexpensive polish by making a paste of fine gilders' whiting and denatured alcohol. However, many of the American commercial manufacturers of silver polish, such as "Gorham," "3-M," "International," and others, now put out silver polishes with a tarnish inhibitor which preserves the natural luster of silver from three to six months. If you live in an area where rapid tarnishing is a problem these products are worth the extra cost.

Electrochemical Method

An electrochemical method frequently recommended for cleaning silver is to soak it in a solution of 1 ounce of washing soda to one pint of distilled water in an old aluminum pan. Lacking such a pan, you may use a glass bowl or an enameled pan which has a sheet or two of crumpled aluminum foil on the bottom. The silver article is immersed until clean, rinsed off in distilled water, and wiped with a soft cloth. This method should not be tried with plated ware since there is a possibility of stripping off the plate.

Dip Cleaner

A dip cleaner may be used, consisting of one ounce of thiourea (from a drug store or photo supply store) dissolved in one pint of distilled water to which have been added 2 or 3 drops of Eastman Kodak's Photo-Flo Solution to make the solution wetter. This treatment is mild, nonabrasive, and is recommended for mild tarnishing. Rinse the object afterwards in distilled water, and dry with a soft cloth.

Know your materials before proceeding with treatment. This metal bowl was glazed with paint to resemble antique bronze. Use of a mild acid solution to clean the surface caused severe etching of the metal (left side of lid). The object was actually a zinc casting rather than bronze.

Special Problems

Urban water often contains chlorine which, while it purifies, has a tendency to cause metal corrosion. Deep-seated corrosion from chlorides and sulphides, or the deposition of copper salts on the surface of the silver, frequently occurs in excavations and underwater sites. In some cases it is desirable to get rid of these encrustations, in some cases part of them represent patinas to be saved. These are such specialized problems that they are not dealt with here, but the reading list includes articles by Plenderleith and others which are recommended for anyone facing such difficulties.

AMBIGUOUS SILVERY-LOOKING MATERIALS

During the nineteenth and early twentieth centuries, new combinations of metal alloys and new methods of coating and plating metals were developed. While objects made of these materials are usually of little interest to the archaeologist—terrestial or marine— many historical societies have nickel-plated stoves, tinned sheet-iron wares, galvanized items, hollow castings, loving cups, firemen's speaking trumpets, and a variety of other things made of silvery-looking metal.

A good rule of thumb in treating such objects is to avoid any chemical cleaners on plated or hot-dipped items for fear of separating the layers. Only the finest polishes should be used because of the danger of wearing off the thin plating. Sheet iron objects, coated with a thin layer of tin or zinc which has worn off in spots, should be protected from humidity as they are particularly vulnerable to rust pits. Any pits should be cleaned mechanically and sealed with wax to hold out moisture. Use a dental pick or some other pointed tool, and work under a low power linen tester lens, to avoid scratching into the uncorroded area.

Many of the silvery-looking art objects and inscribed trophies made around the turn of this century may be of German silver, of a variety of base metals, or of silver plate. Some will polish up nicely with silver polish, and some will be hopeless. If silver polish

115

will not do the job, leave it alone, as stronger treatments or abrasives will only lead to disaster.

Many of the hollow castings so popular in late Victorian and early Edwardian times are made of zinc. Avoid *any* chemical cleaning! Many of them have been given a coat of greenish or dark brown paint to imitate the effect of bronze patina; but turning the casting upside down will usually reveal the bluish white crystalline look of zinc. If parts of these objects are broken off, use adhesive rather than any hot-solder methods to try to mend them.

SUGGESTED READING

Fales, Mrs. Dean A., Jr. "The Care of Antique Silver." *History News* 22 (February, 1967), Technical Leaflet #40.

Organ, R. M. "The Treatment of the St. Ninian's Hanging Bowl Complex." *Studies in Conservation* 4 (May, 1959).

Stambolov, T. "Removal of Corrosion on an 18th Century Silver Bowl." *Studies in Conservation* 11 (February, 1966).

15
Textiles

With such exceptions as wedding gowns and dress uniforms, most old garments found in museum collections have had long, hard-working lives. Rugs, curtains, and blankets, too, are often worn, sun faded, soiled, stained, or moth eaten. Caring for such textiles involves: (1) Cleaning, when it does not adversely affect the strength or color of the object. While there are effective methods for removing soil and many stains, injudicious cleaning may cause shrinkage or distortion, color loss, or bleeding. Proper cleaning, on the other hand, improves the appearance, kills insects, their eggs, and larvae, and removes nutrient materials that attract them. (2) Strengthening weak garments and fabrics by mending tears, filling in losses, and supporting weak areas and points of stress. (3) Protecting the textiles against further deterioration—not only by cleaning or mothproofing and mending, but by proper storage conditions and exhibition care.

CARE OF WOOLENS

All woolen (and feather, hair, and fur) articles must be checked for condition before coming into your storage areas. Clothes moths, carpet beetles, and larvae may remain alive but dormant for several years under even unfavorable conditions; but they can be eliminated by poisons or cleaning.

Cleaning

Before any wet or dry cleaning takes place, all loose dirt must be removed by vacuuming. If an article is thin or fragile, place a piece of plastic screening over it to protect it from fluttering or strain. *Do not beat out dust*—old fabrics cannot take this kind of old-fashioned housewifely enthusiasm.

Wet Cleaning

Many woolens in good condition can be washed safely if proper precautions are taken. Test all colored materials before washing by dropping a bit of water on the various colors to see whether or not they run. Put a piece of clean blotter under the area, and with an eye dropper let a few drops of water go through, and check to see if a color stain has developed on the blotter. (Before you consider the wet cleaning of old rugs, be sure you read the articles relative to this in the reading list. Rugs can present special problems.) If colors show no sign of reacting to water, they may be safely washed in lukewarm water and mild soap flakes or synthetic detergent like Woolite, and then rinsed. Avoid any agitation or heat, which tend to felt and shrink wool fibers. Wet wool should not be hung up to dry, because it is heavy. Instead, lay it out flat on clean toweling, shape it according to the original dimensions, and dry gradually.

The drawback to wet cleaning is that old brittle fibers may be adversely affected by the swelling and shrinking occasioned by washing and drying action. Dry cleaning may be advisable instead.

Dry Cleaning

The traditional solvents used in dry cleaning do not wet the fibers of wool, and yet do dissolve greases, oils, waxes, and resins. Modern dry cleaning solutions often include a small percentage of synthetic detergent and water, in an amount safe for woolens and silks, which increases the range of stains that can be cleaned. If a woolen fabric is old and weak, dry cleaning is now considered the safest method for cleaning it.

Generally most small historical societies will send out their woolens to be cleaned rather than attempting to do it themselves. For your dry cleaner to do a satisfactory job, he must know as much as possible about the age and nature of the stains, the dyestuffs, and trim in the garment. Often arrangements can be made to have your fabrics put through on the first charge before other garments are cleaned.

If you decide that you prefer to do your own dry cleaning, a few precautions are in order:

First, you *must have adequate ventilation.* Solvent fumes in confined spaces can cause dizziness, liver and kidney damage, or even death. Do your dry cleaning out-of-doors on a breezy day.

Second, use a safe solvent with a high flashpoint like Stoddard Solvent 100°F rather than white gasoline and *do not* use any carbon tetrachloride-based cleaners. They are much too dangerous to your

Neglect of storage conditions allowed moths to attack this wool-faced Indian pouch. Not only are the large moth holes unsightly, but they weaken support for the beadwork.

health. Perchloroethylene is a nonflammable cleaner less toxic than carbon tetrachloride, but it does have an adverse effect on rubber and some plastics.

Third, if you are a smoker, don't smoke for a few hours after using these solvents or you will risk an unpleasant bout of nausea. If you are going to be dry cleaning some afternoon, do not have a cocktail for lunch, since alcohol in the bloodstream apparently accelerates any toxic effect the solvent fumes may have. (These points are not a "temperance talk," but rather the results of practical experience.) In view of the uncertainties and problems of home dry cleaning, most curators will find it advantageous to send out their problem pieces to a reliable cleaner who is sympathetic to the museum.

Whether you choose wet or dry cleaning methods, you will rid the garment not only of soil and stains, but of unwanted insects, larvae and eggs. Proper cleaning before storage or exhibition is cheap, practical insurance.

Discouraging and killing unwanted beasties

Cleanliness

Moths like dark, quiet places; thus a periodic airing and sunning of your woolens will tend to discourage them. But woolens must also be clean. It is soil—food, grease, and other like stains—that attracts moths to woolens. Cleaning processes therefore serve the triple purpose of getting rid of unsightly stains, killing larvae and eggs, and removing nutrient materials that would encourage future invasion. Keep your storage areas clean by washing, vacuuming, and brushing to eliminate moth attractants.

Sealed Containers

Cleaned woolens can be safely kept in drums, boxes, chests, or rooms that are sealed—but they must be *tightly* sealed, as larvae can penetrate openings of 1/16″. Use tape seals around boxes and chests and in corners and doors of storage rooms. Even cedar chests are

119

not immune. They tend to deter, but do not kill moths; and carpet beetles are not at all affected by cedar chests.

Poisons

Moth flakes of the naphthalene or paradichlorobenzene variety are effective in closed containers, if the temperature becomes high enough (about 90°F. or so) to turn the flakes into a gas. It is the vapors and not the solids which kill moths. There should be a strong enough concentration of crystals per unit of woolens to be unpleasant to the senses if they are to be effective as a fumigant.

Cyanide gas (hydrogen cyanide) is an effective fumigant for all insects and rodents but will not affect larvae or eggs, and therefore must be used periodically until the trouble is cleared up. UNDER NO CIRCUMSTANCE SHOULD THE MUSEUM WORKER USE THIS MATERIAL HIMSELF. ONE WHIFF IS INSTANTLY FATAL. CYANIDING MUST BE DONE BY SPECIALISTS. Despite its danger to humans and its ability to kill insects only at the adult stage, cyanide gas is extremely useful for materials like furs, native costumes of mixed materials, overstuffed furniture, hidden areas, and materials that cannot be reached by sprays or safely processed by liquid media. An example would be ethnographic materials such as elaborate headdresses made of mud, wood, straw, fur, shell, and feathers, and painted with fugitive pigments.

D.D.T. (dichlorodiphenyltrichloroethane) is considered a bit old-fashioned by some people nowadays, but it has the advantage of being residual and giving long-lasting protection; and it can be applied by the curator or an assistant.

Your dry cleaner can mothproof many items when he cleans them. There are also pest control services which can fumigate your quarters and/or provide periodic inspection and service. But remember that such services cannot take the place of personal care and periodic inspection of the collections by a conscientious curator.

A NOTE ON SILK

Silks should be treated with even more care than woolens. Old silk often becomes quite brittle, and friction or sharp folds will break the fibers. Old silk must be supported and not hung free from walls. Frequently the garment or flag can be couched or stitched between two layers of fine, almost invisible silk or synthetic netting. But determining whether this can be done with a specific piece, and the actual job itself, are for textile experts. During the nineteenth century, silk was sometimes weighted with tin salts to give it more luster. Old dresses and flags so treated eventually fall to fragments and dust; and there is as yet no known way of saving them.

CARE OF COTTON AND LINEN

Since cotton and linen are not affected by moths, and do not felt or shrink to the same degree as wool when washed in hot alkaline cleaning solutions, a proportionally greater amount of these materials survive in museum collections. Unfortunately these materials are often treated in a rather cavalier manner, as if they would last forever. Old curtains are hung up on display indefinitely, until one day when they are taken down for washing it is discovered that they are not only sun faded, but sun rotted, and will fall to pieces in the wash. Give some thought, then, to the care of your cottons and linen.

Unhealthy environment

Exposure to sunlight for a short period can diminish stains and yellowing, but prolonged exposure over weeks and months leads to fading of color and patterns, speeded-up oxidation, and embrittlement of the fiber. On the other hand, darkness, still air, and high humidity lead to the formation of mold growths that discolor and eventually destroy the fabric.

Rust stains

Rust from steel pins, staples, or other sources of contact with iron causes stubborn stains which, in addition to being unsightly, are harmful to the garment.

Mechanical damage

Throwing an old cotton or linen textile in a modern washing machine is asking for broken fibers; use hand-washing methods. Support old fabrics on exhibit by mounting on plastic screening, between Plexiglas sheets, or couch-stitching to silk netting, according to the nature, size, and age of the article. If costumes are to be displayed, there should be padding on the shoulder area of the mount to distribute the weight, since many old garments had only a single shoulder seam instead of a shoulder yoke. Dresses with heavy ruffles should be supported from the waist or pelvic area as well, to relieve the strain of weight on the shoulder seams.

If your museum is in an area of industrial fumes, try to protect the fabrics by covering them with glass or clear plastic. And keep all fabrics—wool, silk, cotton, or linen—out of the reach of women. They cannot resist handling the material. If you do not believe this, ask the manager of a yardgoods store.

CLEANING OF FABRICS IN GENERAL

Stains that are allowed to dry or harden are more difficult to remove than fresh stains. Try to remove all stains or stain-causing materials as quickly as possible; otherwise the stains tend to saturate the fibers. In addition, a dried stain is frequently less soluble than a wet one. For example, latex paint, Elmers "Glue-All," and egg white can all be removed relatively easily while still fresh by rinsing in cold water; but once dried they are stubborn and intractable.

While many "household hints" articles advise pouring boiling hot water on fresh stains, do not use it unless you know what the specific staining agent is, or you may make matters worse. Many protein stains like milk, egg, and blood, plus some dyestuffs, are easily removed with cold water when fresh, but are "set" by hot water and become almost impossible to remove by home methods.

A list of stains and how to remove them is not included here since the reading list gives a number of sources, from inexpensive government pamphlets to complex technical treatments, which include such lists. Most of these are readily available.

Before proceeding with any cleaning method, make sure that you test the fabric (and the various color areas) with whatever solutions you are going to use to be certain that they will not affect the material, the dyestuffs, or the trim. As mentioned earlier, old rugs, especially Oriental ones, are so complex in structure and dyestuffs that they should not be treated by the amateur.

When spot-cleaning woolens with solvents, work spots from the edge to the center in order to minimize rings, put blotters underneath the stain, and use a minimum of solvent.

When bleaching cottons and linen, avoid strong bleaches like Clorox which are difficult to rinse out completely, and which will eventually degrade and weaken fabrics. If you use alkaline bleaches, put a little vinegar in the rinse water to neutralize the effect of the alkali. Do not use alkali bleaches on wool or silk!

As a washing compound for museum cotton and linen, Lux or Ivory soap flakes dissolved in distilled water to which a bit of washing soda has been added is still the most efficient and safest agent. Commercial synthetic detergents often appear to give a "whiter washday white" because they have optical bleaches that respond to the ultraviolet rays of the sun and fluorescent lights. And despite the television commercials, there is no evidence that the currently touted "new enzyme formulas" are any substitute for the soaking of a garment.

If the fabric is old and weak, stitch it temporarily between two pieces of plastic screening, put it in a tray of neutral soap solution, and obtain the cleaning action by tamping it with a sponge, to agitate the solution through the fibers. Follow with one or more rinsings in clear water. If stains remain, allow the wet piece to sit in the sunlight until dry, and you will have done all you safely can. To be sure, there are a variety of stain removers, but they will sometimes remove the stain at the expense of weakening the fabric.

SUGGESTED READING

Bellinger, L. "Basic Habits of Textile Fibres." In *Recent Advances in*

Conservation. London: Butterworths, 1963.
Clear basic information about cotton, linen, wool, and silk—a must for anyone handling textiles.

"Cleaning and Mounting Procedures for Wool Textiles." *Workshop Notes* #1. Textile Museum, 2320 S Street, N.W., Washington, D.C. 20008.

Columbus, J. V. "Washing Techniques." *Bulletin of the AG-IIC* 7:2 (1967).

Delft Conference on the Conservation of Textiles. Collected reprints, 2nd ed. London: International Institute for Conservation, 1964.
An outstanding summary on what is known at present about old textiles and their care.

"Drycleaning." *CIBA Review* (January, 1964).
A historical and technological view.

Finch, K. "Laboratory and Studio Notes—Conservation of a Dress." *Studies in Conservation* 8 (August, 1963).

Gallo, P. "Problems in the Use of Insecticides on Occupied Premises." In *Recent Advances in Conservation*. London: Butterworths, 1963.
A frightening article on the toxicity of various insecticides, what precautions to take, and first aid treatment for insecticide poisoning.

Giffen, Jane C. "Care of Textiles and Costumes: Cleaning and Storage Techniques." *History News* 25 (December, 1970), Technical Leaflet #2.

Geijer, Agnes. "Preservation of Textile Objects." In *Recent Advances in Conservation*. London: Butterworths, 1963.

—————————. "Treatment and Repair of Textiles and Tapestries." *Studies in Conservation* 6 (November, 1961).

Greene, Francine S. "The Conservation of an Historic Robe." *Museum News* 43 (September, 1964): 26-32.
Specific details on the cleaning and repair of an eighteenth century robe—important because it shows how complex the job of treating deteriorated textiles can be.

Leene, J. E. "Restoration and Preservation of Ancient Textiles, and Natural Science." In *Recent Advances in Conservation*. London: Butterworths, 1963.
A general article on the problems of conserving textiles.

Lehman, D. "Conservation of Textiles at the West Berlin State Museum." *Studies in Conservation* 9 (February, 1964).

Martin, A. R. "Drycleaning Museum Textiles." *Bulletin of the AG-IIC* 7:2 (1967).

McLendon, Verda I. "Removing Stains from Fabrics—Home Methods." U.S. Department of Agriculture. Home and Garden Bulletin #62. Washington, D.C.: Government Printing Office, 1959.
A good primer for those with no specialized training.

Plenderleith, Harold J. *The Conservation of Antiquities and Works of Art.* New York: Oxford University Press, 1956. (See pp. 93-115.)

"Preservation of Dated Tiraz Fabrics." *Workshop Notes* #8. The Textile Museum. Can be obtained from the Textile Museum, 2320 S Street, N.W., Washington, D.C. 20008

"Principles of Practical Cleaning for Old and Fragile Textiles." *Workshop Notes* #14. The Textile Museum.

"Procedures for Cleaning Cotton Textiles." *Workshop Notes* #4. The Textile Museum.

Randlett, J. C., and Nicklaw, W. J. *Spotting.* Silver Springs, Md.: National Institute of Dry Cleaning, 1956.
A short title, but this is *the* manual on removing stains from textiles.

Rice, Col. J. W. *Textile Museum Journal* 2:1. (Articles on Textile Conservation)

"Rugs: Preservation, Display and Storage." *Workshop Notes* #5. The Textile Museum.

16
Ceramics

The term "ceramics" refers to a variety of baked-earth materials, ranging from coarse textured Iroquois cooking pots to fine Dresden china figurines. We will include here related materials, such as plaster of Paris busts and chalkware, since they are mended in a similar manner.

VITREOUS CERAMICS

Vitreous ceramics are high-fired, hard glazed, and usually rather thin in cross-section. They are chemically stable, resist the elements, and except for sudden extreme thermal shock (or being dropped) present little problems. Occasionally dust or stains accumulate in a crackled glaze, giving the affected area a brownish discoloration. Washing the area with a strong detergent, followed by application of bleaching strength hydrogen peroxide (sold in drug stores as "20 volume") will bring out as much of the stain as is possible.

When broken, thin ware like porcelain requires a powerful adhesive to give any holding strength. Consequently, the new two-part resins are often used instead of adhesives of the "Duco" and "Ambroid" type, which are acceptable for thicker ware. The disadvantage of the two-part resins is that once set up, they cannot be dissolved. Thus anyone who uses them must plan carefully to be certain that all parts will go together in sequence. It is essential to work with as thin a glue line as is possible. A box filled with clean sand will be helpful for supporting round pots or for putting plates at a convenient angle to glue on a shard and prevent it from moving while drying. A new adhesive "Eastmans 910" (a cyano-acrylate) available from Eastman Organic Chemicals, will cement together very thin pieces with great holding power. It sets up in about 30 seconds when the two pieces are pressed together. Being as thin as water, there is no buildup of heavy glue-lines. It is useful for glass as well as ceramics. It can be dissolved in n-n-dimethyl formamide, also made by Eastman. It currently sells at $10. an ounce, but is worth the cost for tricky or fine pieces that cannot be clamped easily while being mended.

Parts that stick out and have leverage exerted on them (teapot

The principal problem in conservation of pottery is mending breakage.

handle), or small cross-sections that support considerable weight (a figurine balanced on one foot), may need more than just adhesive. Hollow parts may require dowel or wire reinforcement, and handles or spouts may need metal spring cramps for extra support. This kind of repair work is not learned overnight; and for complicated or valuable pieces it would be better to send out the piece to someone that specializes in this work. For those who are interested in knowing about or learning the techniques, the book by Parsons and Curl listed in the suggested readings cannot be equaled.

HIGH-FIRED EARTHENWARES

High-fired, thick-sectioned earthenwares are a joy to the historian and the archaeologist alike. They are reasonably sturdy, and are unaffected by heat, humidity, or insects. Through a study of their design elements, materials, and construction, the scholar can obtain information about past cultures. Given care in storage and handling they should last forever. Even a broken pot (if there are a reasonable number of contiguous shards) can be reconstructed through the aid of templates, to give the archaeologist or student the form of the original vessel. The detailed article by Eldon Wolff mentioned in the reading list will give complete information.

MENDING POTTERY

Two important points must be observed in mending pottery: be certain that the edges of the shards are clean, dry, and free from grit; and work with as thin a glue line as possible. Errors tend to be cumulative. Start with a definite area if possible, like base or rim shards, and watch your sequence. Sometimes it is necessary to put the pieces together with tape or a temporary glue, number and photograph them and then give a final gluing. Nothing is more irritating than finding out that the last shard will not fit.

A suitable adhesive should remain tacky long enough to enable correct alignment of the shards; it should dry thin and hard; and it should be easily dissolved again if one botches the job. Remember

127

to have a sandbox for such mending operations, so odd-shaped pieces can be held at a proper angle or propped temporarily while the adhesive is drying.

Missing areas can be built up with plaster of Paris, Hydrostone, or Durham's "Rock Hard Putty." Back up the gap with nonhardening modeling clay. Then fill the area with the plaster. Pour enough material so that it is slightly raised above the surface, as there may be some shrinkage in drying. The excess may be worked down with a rasp or sculptor's riffle file, a knife, or sandpaper. But do be careful not to scratch the original pottery.

The philosophy of tinting mended areas varies among institutions and archaeologists. Some leave the plaster areas white in order to prevent confusion as to what is original. Others put a slight amount of dry powder color in with the plaster mix; and still others try, on aesthetic grounds, to match the background as exactly as possible. The choice will be determined by the needs of your institution and the philosophy of the curator or director. Should you decide to tint reconstructed areas, you may use oil or water colors, though the newer artists' colors made of acrylic emulsions like "Liquitex" or "Hyplar" will prove easier in the long run. They do not change in tint upon drying or aging, and they can be made matte or shiny. Do not become discouraged if you cannot get an exact match in color—you will discover that even a "simple" color like brown seems to have 16,000 variations, and even the experts do not always hit the correct combination on the first try. However, if you can tint the filled-in areas enough that they are not noticeable at five feet distance, it will be sufficient to remove the curse of otherwise white plaster-patch areas.

SPECIAL PROBLEMS

Soft-fired pottery and salt-laden or friable coarse wares from archaeological sites present problems of their own. Frequently there will be limy deposits which obscure the design. If the pottery is hard and strong the lime can be scrubbed off with a fiber brush in a solution of 95% water and 5% concentrated hydrochloric acid, and then rinsed. If, however, the pottery is soft, or has chalk or marble or limestone grit in it, it should not be cleaned in acid lest the material decompose.

Even washing may cause low-fired or friable wares to go to pieces. If it is necessary to wash the pieces in order to remove salts, the pot (or shards) should first be coated with soluble nylon dissolved in alcohol (available from TALAS) or "Duco" or "Ambroid" thinned with acetone or amyl acetate. After this coating has dried the pieces may be safely soaked in water to remove excess salts.

Because edges of pottery in this category are so soft and/or friable, extra care must be taken in assembling them. Often dipping the edges in a thinned solution of adhesive will penetrate just deeply enough to consolidate the edges. Then when dry they can be put together with full strength adhesive. If the edges fit together poorly because of crumbling or wear, an adhesive with filler properties may be needed. But be certain that the two shards do belong side-by-side. Don't grind them to fit.

Gluing potshards together is quite easy—but ending up with a completed pot that fits correctly is not so easy. Don't be discouraged. Work "tight," and proceed slowly.

SUGGESTED READING

Clarke, D. C. *Molding and Casting, Its Technique and Application*. Butler, Md.: The Standard Arts Press, 1946.
Casting in a variety of materials to duplicate or build up parts; methods of coloring and finishing. This book is apparently in the process of revision, so you may be able to obtain a revised edition.
Klein, William Karl. *Repairing, and Restoring China and Glass: The Klein Method*. New York: Harper and Row, 1962.
While the author promises to reveal "many heretofore closely guarded secrets," none of the adhesives, cements, or molding compounds are mentioned by name, but only by code numbers (useful only if you purchase these materials at the author's shop). There are some interesting techniques revealed, but also some drastic surgical and amputation techniques, which would not be acceptable in a museum.

Since the book is addressed primarily to the "amateur, hobbyist, collector and housewife," one should be aware of this philosophical approach.

Parsons, Claudia S. M. and Curl, F. H. *China Mending and Restoration*. London: Faber and Faber, 1963.

See also the section on glass. Highly recommended.

Wheeler, Mortimer. "The Pottery Shed." In *Archaeology from the Earth*. Baltimore, Md.: Penguin Books, Pelican Book A 356, 1964. Chapter 13.

Wilson, Shari. "Restoring Pottery." *Lore* (Winter, 1967). Published by the Milwaukee Public Museum, Wisconsin.

A good practical set of working instructions, plus a list of equipment needed.

Wolff, Eldon. "Pottery Restoration." *Curator* 3:1 (1960): 75-87.

A practical working procedure, particularly for archaeologists who are trying to conjecture the shape of a pot from a limited number of shards.

17
Glass

Glass in the traditional sense is silica which has been fused with potash or soda ash. "Potash" or "ash" refers to the crude alkaline carbonate salts that were extracted by leaching hardwood ash and evaporating the resulting solution. The addition of a small percentage of lime, either deliberately or as an impurity in the ash, gave the glass stability. The inclusion of minute amounts of metallic oxides gave glass color—for example, purple from manganese and green from iron. The mixture was heated until liquefied, was formed, and then allowed to cool and stiffen; and, if the proportion of materials was in correct balance, the result was a stable glass.

Sometime in the seventeenth century it was discovered that if lead oxide were substituted for lime, the resulting glass, while softer, had a clear color and was brighter looking than the potash-lime glass. This was known variously as lead glass, flint glass, or crystal glass and proved to be quite stable. But because it was more expensive than potash-lime glass it was not used for common wares.

DEVITRIFIED GLASS

Early glass makers wanted a clear glass, so they often leached the ashes to purify them. Frequently, as a result, most of the lime content was washed out and the glass became sensitive to moisture. An imperfect mixture of materials or incorrect proportions (such as an excess of lime) could also lead to gradual deterioration of the glass.

Glass is a stiff liquid rather than a crystalline solid; and under certain conditions, such as thermal or humidity change, elements of the glass in an object which has been made of an unbalanced mixture will begin to devitrify (return to a crystalline form). Depending on the amount of devitrification the appearance of the glass will vary. It may appear cloudy or, as is sometimes seen in historical excavations, the glass may appear iridescent and quite beautiful. In conditions of low humidity this glass is reasonably stable.

Soda ash or potash glass that is deficient in lime is extremely hygroscopic, and as the salts pull moisture from the air, the condition known as "weeping glass" develops. This type of glass is extremely unstable unless immediate preservative steps are taken.

Before

Devitrified glass and weeping glass should be kept under as dry storage conditions as possible, even if it means air tight containers with silica gel as a moisture absorber.

One method of drying weeping glass involves the use of weak sulphuric acid baths followed by rinsing and drying in alcohol-ether baths. Consult Plenderleith's book for specific directions. The treatment does not stop the process but only slows it down, since the problem is an inherent defect in the original formulation of the glass.

BROKEN GLASS

Another problem facing the conservator is broken glass. Fractured edges are not only thin in cross-section as a rule, but they present extremely smooth surfaces. All adhesive directions, even for the "miracle all-purpose" types, say in small print "be sure to roughen surfaces before applying adhesive." This is more easily said than done when working with pieces of a crystal goblet. Solvent-type glues like "Seal-All" and "Duco" have relatively little holding strength when used on thin edges. On pieces where there are heavy cross-sections, they may not dry out for an almost interminable time because the solvent is trapped between two nonporous surfaces.

Some glass may be so fragile and/or so shattered that it is not practical for an amateur to mend. If mending is attempted, generally the only adhesives that will possibly hold are two-part resins, like epoxy or polyester resins. (See page 126 for reference to Eastman 910.) Just remember that they are nonreversible—be sure you have a tight fit and thin glue lines, because you have no second chance.

Broken glass should be thoroughly clean and dry before you attempt to mend it. Synthetic detergent, alcohol, or acetone may be used, according to the nature of the dirt, oil, or grease stain.

When using two-part adhesives, observe the working time or "pot-life" given on the label. In this way you will know how long you have to work on a piece before the adhesive sets. Avoid getting these resins on your hands, as most of them are irritating to the skin. Upon request, the Corning Museum of Glass, Corning, New York, will send you a mimeographed pamphlet dealing with adhesives

132

Oil and vinegar cruet, broken in several pieces, could be mended adequately because the cross-section of the glass was relatively thick.

After

for glass and molding resins for filling in missing parts.

ORGANIC DEPOSITS

Organic deposits inside bottles, like dried wine, dried milk or cream, often may be removed by soaking the bottle overnight in a solution of "Calgon" plus a bit of detergent. Next day with the bottle about half-full of this mixture, pour in some air rifle shot (steel BB's from any hardware store) roll them around the sides loosening the deposits, and then rinse. *Be careful* that you roll the shot around rather than shaking it. Shaking could easily crack fragile glassware. If the glass is extremely thin, do not attempt this trick, but remove as much as you can with a bristle brush.

SUGGESTED READING

Parsons, Claudia S. M., and Curl, F. H. *China Mending and Restoration.* London: Faber and Faber, 1963.
A conservative, well-illustrated, lucid book on the techniques of mending china and glass. Stresses skill, restraint, and conserving, rather than restoring or altering, or excessive over-painting. Gives specific names of materials used, and their virtues and limitations.
Werner, A. E. "The Care of Glass in Museums." *Museum News* 44 (June, 1966), Technical Supplement #13.

18
Bone, Ivory, and Teeth

IDENTIFYING BONE, IVORY, OR TEETH

These materials can be difficult for the layman to identify, particularly when they have been sawed, carved, stained, or otherwise altered from their original shape. Considering that material like narwhal tusk was often dyed in a variety of colors by the Chinese; or that there are ambiguous terms like "whalebone," which usually refers not to the actual bone, but to the food strainer (baleen)— the dark, flexible, fringed sheets found in the mouth of the right whale or baleen whale—it is no wonder that identification is complex. The illustrated monograph by Penniman will be useful for those who may have difficulty in identifying certain materials of this category.

Ivory, teeth, and tusks contain a hard dense core of dentine with a fine longitudinal grain structure, and have an outer coating of enamel; whereas bone is somewhat softer and of a coarser cellular structure. Despite this workaday definition, until you have worked with these materials a good deal, there will still be pieces that give you doubts. If you are dealing with skeletal material but are uncertain whether these are the long bones of a camel or of a horse, or the skull of a groundhog or of a beaver, any local college zoology department should be able to help with identification or bibliographical sources.

CARE OF THESE MATERIALS

Although these materials are relatively stable, they can be decomposed by acids and are degraded or cracked by prolonged exposure to heat and water, or by burial in damp soil. The softer ossein, or organic part, is quickly decomposed by exposure to water or burial; in some instances it is replaced by salts or becomes mineralized.

Avoid having objects exhibited in sunlight, in areas of high temperature, such as near heat pipes or ducts, or in closed cases with multiple incandescent bulbs.

Warped pieces

It is sometimes suggested that such pieces be soaked in vinegar or dilute phosphoric acid in order to soften and straighten out the objects. But because acids degrade the material and alter the surface, this procedure is not recommended. Learn to live with the piece as is.

Grease spots

Usually a mild petroleum solvent like benzine applied with a cotton swab will do the trick. If the grease has sunk in, make a poultice of the benzine and fuller's earth and allow it to stand awhile on the area affected.

Stains

Porous, bony material is easily stained by metallic corrosion products, paints, dyes, and other organic materials. The only safe bleach to attempt is hydrogen peroxide (20 volume) with a few drops of ammonia added per half-pint of peroxide. If this does not work, do not attempt stronger bleaches; they are usually aqueous, strongly alkaline, or acid, and therefore destructive.

Washing

Washing bone and ivory is not generally recommended, especially if the objects are old or cracked, since it is almost impossible to remove the water from cells or deep striations, and warping may result. A dry bristle brush or tooth brush is safe for removing loose dirt. If further treatment is necessary, a piece of cottonwool dampened in a detergent solution may be rubbed over the surface. This should be followed by dry swabs to soak up any moisture. Do not allow the objects to become wet or to sit in water.

The exception to this rule would be objects from marine sites, where they have been impregnated with salts. These should be leached out in successive baths of fresh water, and the water then dried out by successive baths of denatured alcohol. After this has been done, the specimen may be treated with a coating of a synthetic

Care must be taken to keep weak skeletal materials intact as they are removed from excavations.

resin varnish like polyvinyl acetate. (For other variants on safely removing salts, see the following discussion of "Consolidation.")

CONSOLIDATION OF FRIABLE BONE FROM EXCAVATIONS

Frequently bone artifacts or skeletal materials will be so weak that they cannot be removed from a site without being strengthened. If the bony material is damp, dilute emulsions of polyvinyl acetate (50/50 in water) may be brushed on while the material is still *in situ*. Two or three layers, with drying intervals in between, will usually be enough to enable safe removal of small animal and human bones. (Easily available commercial brands of polyvinyl acetate emulsions are sold in most hardware stores and lumberyards as carpenters' white glues—"Le-Page's," "Elmer's Glue-All," etc.) Larger bones may need an additional reinforcement of bandages and glue, or for quite large ones layers of burlap bags soaked in fresh plaster of Paris may be necessary. Lacking even these materials, a papier maché may be improvised by soaking strips of Kraft paper bags in flour paste and applying several layers.

Some bone specimens may be not only weak but also full of salt encrustations which must be washed out. You may need to hold the object together with an adhesive that is permeable to water so that the consolidated object can be soaked in a water bath. "Ambroid," a cellulose nitrate-based adhesive, or a coating of 5% soluble nylon dissolved in denatured alcohol may be used.

Bone that is weak but free from dirt, water, or salts may be consolidated by the aforementioned adhesives, by the traditional shellac in alcohol, by solutions of polyvinyl acetate ("Vinylite AYAF" from Union Carbide) or by butylmethacrylates (Elvacite 2046 from DuPont, Polychemical Division). In a pinch, some of the generally available but expensive spray synthetic resin varnishes like "Krylon," which are found in any hardware store, may be used.

A NOTE ON HORN

This is a tough water and heat resistant material under normal

136

conditions, and it will usually take a prolonged exposure to a combination of heat and moisture to warp or degrade it. But horn is susceptible to the attacks of various types of beetles, and if infestation is suspected, fumigation is in order. A colleague of mine has observed that pieces of horn inlay or decorative work on old weapons shrink slightly with age. Under such circumstance they are best left alone, as no soaking or rejuvenating techniques will re-enlarge their dimensions.

SUGGESTED READING

Penniman, T. K. *Pictures of Ivory and Other Animal Teeth, Bone, and Antler.* Oxford: Oxford University Press, 1962.
    Magnified photos which show how to differentiate among these often confused materials. Primarily useful for identification.
Peterson, Mendel. *History Under the Sea: A Manual for Underwater Exploration.* Rev. ed. Washington, D.C.: Smithsonian Institution Press, 1969. (See pp. 32 and 63.)
Plenderleith, Harold L. *The Conservation of Antiquities and Works of Art.* New York: Oxford University Press, 1956.
    Chapter 6, "Bone and Ivory."
Recent Advances in Conservation. London: Butterworths, 1963. (See pp. 127-28.)

19
Stone

PROBLEMS OF STONE CARE

It would seem that an inorganic substance like stone would be one class of material that would be free from decay. Yet a look at diseased and acid-pitted stone facades in industrial cities, half-obliterated lettering on gravestones, and eroding coastal cliffs should convince anyone that even stone is susceptible to damage by water, frost, smoke, chemical fumes, various acids, and salts.

Statuary or other stone artifacts that are porous, crumbly, or rough-textured should not be exposed to the elements. Water and/or frost can accumulate in small pitted areas, causing spalling or cracking of the objects. Even so seemingly innocuous a substance as dew is extremely destructive. Since each drop contains dissolved carbon dioxide gas, it forms a weak solution of carbonic acid which is particularly inimical to such materials as mortar, concrete, chalk, limestone, and marble. These materials are commonly used for construction, statuary, and monuments so it is not surprising that many of them have weathered badly. This is especially noticeable in cities such as St. Louis or Gary, where sulphurous fumes combine with moisture to produce new acid combinations.

CLEANING STONE

Marble is probably the most common stone found in museums. Marble may be cleaned by washing in clear water. If further cleaning power is needed, detergent rather than soap should be used.

Rust spots

Rust spots must not be cleaned by the usual acid rust removers, as these will eat marble and limestone. Special reducing agents are available through statuary supply houses and monument works or marble companies.

Organic stains

To remove organic stains like coffee, ink, or tobacco, cover the area for a few hours with a paste made of whiting and 20 volume

hydrogen peroxide. Rinse and examine the spot; try again if necessary.

Oil and grease stains

Wash in aqua ammonia, but watch the fumes! Flood the area
afterwards with hot water, and follow this treatment with a 50/50
mixture of amyl acetate and acetone mixed with whiting to form a
poultice. Cover the spot with foil or some other material to keep
the solvents from evaporating too quickly. After this procedure, wash
the area once more with hot water.

CONSOLIDATION OF STONE

Burnt stone

Burnt stone is commonly found in fireplaces, where either the lime
mortar or the marble or limestone mantel has been reduced by heat
to a crumbly, sugary texture. This effect is similar to the process of
burning limestone, marble, or seashells for quicklime. Their carbon
dioxide content is driven off and a powder of calcium oxide remains.
Attempts to give strength back to the crumbly stone have been made
by repeatedly applying slacked lime in water to the stone, followed
by solutions of soluble casein. A new experimental method utilizing
barium solutions seems to give promise of better results. Once it is
time-tested it may well prove a practical answer, but as yet neither
of these methods is foolproof.

Crumbly surfaces can be consolidated by impregnation in a hot
wax bath. The item should soak long enough to be certain that the
heat and wax penetrate into the deepest recesses. High-strength
resins and adhesives are not generally recommended because they
usually have an objectionable gloss, and if the material is very
crumbly or has cleavage planes, the new synthetic skin may tend
to pull and thus spall off pieces of original material.

Salts

Salts can be leached out of materials such as adobe, soft sedi-
mentary rocks, mud, and colored earth murals by coating the ma-

Deteriorating tombstones show results of
exposure to natural elements.

terials with soluble nylon dissolved in alcohol. Being permeable
to water, the thin layer of nylon acts as a consolidant for the surface but at the same time lets water enter the pores of the stone.
The object is soaked in periodic changes of fresh water until the
salts are removed, and the object is then air dried. Since soluble
nylon has less surface tension than many stronger synthetic resins,
it will protect the surface of the material but not exert enough force
to cause spalling.

Encrustations

Lichens, limy encrustations, or old mortar can be removed from
potshards, some stone, and brick with a dilute solution of hydrochloric acid (add 5 volumes of concentrated hydrochloric acid to 95
volumes of water. Remember to add the acid to the water and not
vice versa.) Soak the article in the solution until the fizzing stops;
or if it is too large, scrub on the solution with a vegetable fiber
brush. Wear rubber gloves, rubber apron, and goggles when working with an acid, especially if you are scrubbing vertical surfaces.
After the acid has done its work, flush off the area with lots and lots.
of clean water. Since hydrochloric acid dissolves limy materials, do
not use it on limestone, marble, or any stone or ceramic materials
containing lime.

SUGGESTED READING

Conservation of Stone and Wooden Objects. London: International Insti-
tute for Conservation, 1970. Reprints from the New York IIC con-
ference.
Plenderleith, Harold L. *The Conservation of Antiquities and Works of Art.*
New York: Oxford University Press, 1956.
Part 3, "Siliceous and Related Materials."

APPENDICES

Appendix I–Adhesives

There are thousands of adhesives on the market today capable of joining almost any combination of materials under a great variety of circumstances. But no one adhesive product can do all jobs, no matter how optimistic their promotional literature sometimes seems. It is impossible to list all the adhesives on the market by trade names —instead this discussion is a guide to the qualities of generally available types of adhesives.

Before using any unfamiliar adhesive, always read the label or the accompanying literature to be sure it meets your specific need. Or, if you cannot find an adhesive locally that will do what you want, write the manufacturer for technical literature. Most companies are quite obliging in this respect if you write using your institution's letterhead. If you feel that you would be overwhelmed by technical descriptions, ask the manufacturer for a specific recommendation for your problem. But you must provide as clear and detailed information as possible in requesting an appropriate adhesive. The following are some of the pertinent questions to consider in deciding what adhesive you need.

1. What specific materials will be joined? It is not enough to say, "cloth to metal"; say "linen canvas to stainless steel," or whatever the case may be.

2. Will you have a tight fit, or do you need an adhesive with filler qualities to compensate for two irregular surfaces with some voids? Remember most adhesives work best where the glue line is thin. Casein glue is about the only common exception; but it may not be otherwise suitable for your specific job, as it causes staining of some hardwoods, is not waterproof, and does not join some materials.

3. Do you want a rigid or a flexible bond? You may want an adhesive or caulking compound that will allow for dimensional changes in materials as a result of varying temperature and humidity changes. (Problems with wooden boats or leaking skylights are good examples of these conditions.)

4. How will the article be used—in a static exhibit, or out-of-doors in live demonstrations? In other words, what is the range of specific

143

thermal, climatic, and physical stresses, solvents, chemicals, and vapors to which you expect it to be subjected, either intermittently or continually?

5. How strong or permanent an adhesive is necessary? Do you want the repair to last forever or should the job be reversible if some of the pieces are not properly mated? Some adhesives are insoluble once they have set; while others may be soluble, but the solvent could harm the object. For example, removing adhesive soluble in alcohol and acetone from a piece of woodenware would cause no difficulty unless the piece were polychromed in a medium sensitive to these solvents. Test all of your materials before you proceed.

6. Under what conditions will the adhesive be applied—indoors in a warm room, in an unheated shed, in outdoor cold, or underwater? Many adhesives will not work well above or below a certain temperature and humidity range.

7. Do you want to apply the adhesive as a liquid for better penetration into joints or porous areas, or as a stiffer gel that will adhere to vertical or overhead surfaces?

8. What tools will you use to apply it—your fingers, a stick, brush, trowel, caulking gun, spatula, spray-gun, or roller? Some adhesives may affect certain types of bristles, are discolored by certain metals, clog spray guns, or affect the skin.

9. How long a working time (pot life) is necessary, or how quickly do you want the work to set up? Remember you can get "instant bond" or overnight hardening; each method has its own advantages and liabilities.

10. Finally, an important but often overlooked point: what is the shelf- or storage-life of the adhesive? There is no point to buying a year's supply if its storage life is only three months, or if it begins to break down in the jar after it has first been used and exposed to air. This is a tricky business; many of the two-part synthetic resins and rubber molding compounds have a shelf life guaranteed from three to six months. This will vary with the product, although the life can often be extended for a few months by storing the adhesives in a refrigerator.

There would be less of a problem if all the containers were date-stamped, or if one could buy small amounts directly from the maker. But one usually buys from a local merchant; and there is no way of knowing how long the product has been on his shelf. Buy as small amounts as are consistent with your anticipated needs over the next few months. Then write on the container the month and year you purchased it. At least you will know how long it's been on your shelf.

Test the adhesive for setting-up time each time before you use it on an artifact. Some of the amino-resin adhesives that have become too old will simply make a gritty, watery curd which can be washed or wiped off the object again. But—when your two-part epoxy or polyester resins become old, all sorts of interesting but unpleasant things can happen. They may remain sticky and not set up at all, in which case you have an almost hopeless job of removing the substance again, especially from porous surfaces. On the other hand, I have also had the experience of old batches setting up *solid* during the mixing process. Think what this would mean if you had two adhesive-covered surfaces only half-positioned together at the time the resin set up! For practical purposes removal of a hardened two-part resin is almost impossible without great danger to the object. So beware—test your adhesives on trial bits of material first!

ADHESIVE SUBSTANCES THAT CAN CAUSE TROUBLE

Pressure-Sensitive Cellulose Tape. This type of tape is most familiarly known as "Scotch" tape, a name which correctly applies to only one of several tapes manufactured by 3M Company. The ordinary brand of cellulose tapes one buys at dime stores and hardware stores degrades in storage or in use, bonds poorly over a long period of time, and often leaves permanent stains on paper. There are transparent mending tapes which are considered safe for paper, and these are available from library supply companies.

Pressure-Sensitive Laminating Film. This resembles cellulose tape in appearance, but comes in sheets or wide rolls, and is highly touted (by the makers) for preserving "valuable documents, drivers' licenses, cherished photos, etc." Personal experiments with these materials have convinced me that they would be disastrous on valuable items. The films degraded in a few months of storage, stuck only partially to the objects to be laminated, and were far more difficult to remove with solvents than even common cellulose tape. (See pp. 67-8.)

Dry-Mounting Tissue. Either wax- or shellac-based, these are used with heat and pressure to mount documents and photographs. When used with a proper dry-mounting press these tissues are useful for mounting photographs or labels for exhibitions. But, because they can sometimes stain or become difficult to remove safely, dry-mounting tissues are *not* recommended for mounting original prints and documents. Confine their use to temporary mounting of duplicatable exhibition materials.

Rubber Cement. This adhesive should not be given houseroom. It stains paper quite badly and often permanently; and even though its adhesive quite commonly fails in use, the part you wish to remove is almost impossible to dissolve. It is not even recommended for exhibition use, and definitely not in the field of conservation.

Spray-Can Adhesives. These are used on one or both surfaces of materials to be mounted, depending on whether a temporary or permanent job is desired. When the adhesive is dry the two pieces are put together. As with contact cements the positioning must be exact, because once stuck together the pieces cannot be wiggled around. Often rubber-based, these adhesives in spray-can form also seem to suffer from the same defects as old-fashioned rubber cement: sometimes they hold like fury; other times they fail. They may possibly be useful for exhibition work, but not for conservation.

Contact Cement. These are also related to rubber cements and spray-can adhesives in that they all presumably have a latex base. Since they all may have sulphur in them, these adhesives should not be used in exhibition areas where there may be lead or silver artifacts which can be adversely affected.

Library Paste. The commercial varieties have preservatives which are acidic and should not be used for paper conservation, as the paper will become degraded as a result. Neutral wheat pastes can be purchased from TALAS, Technical Library Service.

Commercial Liquid Animal Hide Glues. These are easier to use than the home made ones; but it is their only advantage. They are inferior in strength to the ones you prepare yourself.

ADHESIVES USEFUL IN THE FIELD OF CONSERVATION

Wheat or Rye Paste. Such neutral starch pastes are dry powders mixed with water. Some are ready-cooked, and some need to be boiled first. They are safer than commercial pastes, but make them in small amounts, for they will not keep so long. They are useful for paper and cardboard because they hold well but can still be safely removed if desired. They are not strong enough for wood or metal.

Filler Compounds. There are many of these on the market. The traditional ones like gesso, spachtle (spackle), putty, and wood fillers are made of inert materials like whiting, plaster, or wood dust, plus an adhesive. These are all useful for filling holes and cracks or for building up missing areas, and they adhere well to clean surfaces. They generally have little bonding strength, however, and are not a substitute for adhesives. Some of the newer fillers, usually two-part resins plus metal powder or fiberglass fillers, do have bonding strength, but they are considerably more expensive. Plan in advance which type you need.

Mastics and caulking compounds act as fillers and adhesives, and are particularly useful when nonporous materials like glass and metal are to be joined. If there are irregularities in the two surfaces, the mastic will fill in to give a more complete holding surface. Caulking mastics also give you the opportunity to wiggle or position the objects into place, a distinct advantage over contact cements. But some of these compounds contain sulphur, and some are difficult to remove once dry. Check the instructions before using them, and experiment.

Animal Glues. Included in this category are fish glue, rabbit-skin glue, gelatin, and hide glue (carpenter's glue)—all traditional glues and still useful. Gelatin by itself or mixed into gesso is still used in fine arts conservation. While ready-made liquid glue is available, ground hide glue is the better material for serious cabinet-work. It is more trouble because the dry glue must be soaked first, then heated, and used while still hot; but this nuisance is more than offset by the fact that it is far stronger than ready-made glue, and unlike some other adhesives it will not stain wood. Where you have tight-fitting joints and the object is not subjected to high moisture, hot hide glue is still among the best and cheapest adhesives.

White Glues (water-resin emulsions). These are among the handiest of the newer adhesives which have come on the market since World War II. They are useful for a variety of porous materials, available everywhere, and reasonably inexpensive. They are nontoxic to the skin, can be thinned with water if desired, and give a good bond. But they should not be used where they will be subjected to steam or high moisture conditions, nor with paper artifacts because of their presumed acidity, nor with metal which they will corrode. White glue is an easily applied and relatively satisfactory adhesive in situations where you might use carpenter's glue but do not want to take the time to prepare it. However, once white glues have dried they are no longer water soluble; usually a mixture of water plus acetone will be necessary to dissolve the bond. Be sure that the object you glue will not be affected by this mixture if disassembly should be necessary.

Clear Adhesives of Soluble Resins. This includes an enormous number of adhesives, most of which are labeled as "all-purpose, mends anything." Generally it is a resin in a quick-evaporating solvent ("Duco" cement is an example). The solid component may be a cellulose product, a vinyl-or acrylic-resin, soluble nylon, etc. Such adhesives are all theoretically capable of being redissolved in their original solvents, although exceptions may occur under certain circumstances. Although neither as strong nor as permanent as two-part resins, they are quite useful for mending pottery or glass since the adhesive can be removed in the event of a poor fit. As a rule, soluble resin adhesives should not be used on large areas because their solvents usually evaporate so quickly that part of the adhesive will be dry before the whole area has been covered. However, in situations where you cannot tie or clamp the pieces together and must hold them by hand, the rapid drying is an advantage. These adhesives are not recommended for fastening together two pieces of nonporous materials of any appreciable surface because the entrapped solvent will cause a weak bond. Remember when using these adhesives that the solvents in most of them are toxic and/or explosive, so take precautions to have ventilation and to allow no naked flames or lit cigarettes.

Melted Waxes and Resins. Stick shellac, beeswax, and various natural resin-wax mixtures have been used for centuries as mending materials; and along with newer synthetic resins and waxes they are still valuable in the conservation field today. Because of the variety of formulae and materials now available, one who wishes to keep up with this field should subscribe to the publications of the International Institute for Conservation of Historic and Artistic Works, which from time to time give reports of experiments in the use of these materials.

Two-Part Synthetic Resins. Typified by resorcinol, epoxy or polyester, these are strong, waterproof permanent adhesives, consisting of a resin plus a hardener and/or catalyst. They can be compounded in an endless number of ways. Since most adhesives of this class cannot be dissolved once they have set, be sure that the pieces to be mended will *never* need to be taken apart again. Think twice.

These resins may be as thin as water so that they can be soaked into dry-rotted wood in ship bilges or into worm-riddled sculpture, or they may be the consistency of syrup, paste, or putty. Some are formulated to remain hard at elevated temperatures; others are made to be flexible at below-freezing levels. A variant of two-part resins is the type in which both materials are pre-mixed in powder form and the user simply adds the proper amount of water and stirs. These have a longer shelf life (one to two years) than most two-part liquid resins, are stronger than white glues, and more moisture resistant. They are usually sold under the general name of "plastic resin glues."

The foregoing is an indication of the varied types of adhesives that are available. Remember: there is no one all-purpose adhesive, even with the newer so-called "miracle glues." The proper adhesive —one that will resist a specified temperature, physical stress, chemical, or solvent action—does exist; and you can find it *if* you spell out your needs to the manufacturers, rather than merely grabbing the nearest "all-purpose" adhesive off your dealer's shelf.

It is a sound idea to keep a record of how various adhesives worked (or failed) for you under certain circumstances. So many of these products may be used in different ways according to the amount of solvent in them or the manner in which they are used—as a protective coating or varnish, as a filler, an adhesive, or a combination. But no adhesive does its best when applied to surfaces that are dirty, dusty, oily, or corroded. A *clean,* roughened surface is usually essential, plus pressure or clamping to hold the pieces immobile until the adhesive is dry. One last word: do be aware that there are new brand names on the market every month; and that even old brands may change their formulation—sometimes for better or sometimes for worse for your particular problem. Make a point of testing new adhesives before using them on valued pieces.

SUGGESTED READING

Synthetic Materials Used In the Conservation of Cultural Property. International Centre for the Study of the Preservation and the Restoration of Cultural Property, 256 Via Cavour, Rome, Italy, 1963.
   A description of various new synthetic resins and other materials used

as varnishes, adhesives, etc. In addition to giving the scientific name of a product, it also gives the trade names and sources of supply in the U.S. and Europe.

Boustead, W. "Conservation of Australian Aboriginal Bark Paintings." *Studies in Conservation* 10 (November, 1966).

Gorton, E. "Restoration of an 18th Century Writing Table." *Studies in Conservation* 6 (February, 1961).

Kostrov and Sheinina. "Restoration of Monumental Painting on Loess Plaster Using Synthetic Resins." *Studies in Conservation* 6 (August, 1961).

Kozlowski, R. "An Apparatus for Glueing Split Panels." *Studies in Conservation* 7 (November, 1962).

Sekino, M. "Restoration of the Great Buddha Statue at Kamakura." *Studies in Conservation* 10 (May, 1965).

The five references listed above represent a cross-section of articles on the application of adhesives to be found in *Studies in Conservation*. If, as a non-member you wish individual issues, address inquiries to: IIC, 608 Grand Bldgs., Trafalgar Square, London, WC2N, 5HN, England.

Gettens and Stout. *Painting Materials, A Short Encyclopedia.* New York: Dover Publications, 1966.

Contains among other information a large and useful section on adhesives, their nature and use. At $2.00 this book is a "must" which any student of conservation can afford.

Macbeth and Strohlein. "The Use of Adhesives in Museums." *Museum News* (May, 1965). Technical Supplement #7.

A definition of various adhesives, plus some specific formulae.

Plenderleith, Harold J. *The Conservation of Antiquities and Works of Art.* New York: Oxford University Press, 1956.

Handbook of Organic Industrial Solvents. Chicago: National Association of Mutual Casualty Companies, 20 North Wacker Drive, 1958.

A list of solvents, some of which you may use in conservation, and their toxicity and flammability ratings.

Appendix II–Abrasives

A SIZE NUMBER COMPARISON OF COMMON ABRASIVE PAPERS

Aluminum oxide Carborundum Garnet	Flint	Emery	Nontechnical description
7/0–240 grit	5/0		Very fine
6/0–220 grit	4/0		Very fine
	3/0		Fine
5/0–180 grit		3/0	Fine
4/0–150 grit	2/0	2/0	Fine
3/0–120 grit		1/0	Fine
	1/0		Medium
2/0–100 grit			Medium
1/0– 80 grit		1	Medium
	1		Medium coarse
1/2– 60 grit		1 1/2	Medium coarse
1 – 50 grit	1 1/2	2	Medium coarse

"Flint" paper or common sandpaper is the cheapest abrasive paper on the market, but it loads up quickly and does not cut so well as the newer ones. It has its place in sanding off old paint, which will load up and waste the more expensive papers.

Modern abrasive papers based on grits like garnet, carborundum, and aluminum oxide, sometimes known as "production papers" or "cabinet paper," are somewhat more expensive than flint paper, but cut faster and do not load up. They can be used on metal as well as wood.

Emery or corundum, a form of aluminum oxide (now made artificially) that was traditionally used for abrading or polishing metal, glass, etc.

Silicon carbide, almost as hard as diamond, is used for abrading and polishing iron, steel, etc. and for finishing lacquer surfaces. Ranging from 200 grits up to the 400's, they are known also as "Tri-M-ite Wet or Dry" papers.

Rottenstone and "000" pumice are traditional natural grits, usually used in a carrier like water or sweet oil for furniture finishing.

Steel wool, ranges in grades from "0000" (occasionally to be found in still finer grades) to "#3." According to the fineness it can be used for everything from high gloss finishes down to removal of rust or of paint or varnishes. The finer grades are highly flammable. The slivers of steel wool can be inhaled easily, can cut through the skin, catch in clothing, and clog up machinery or moving parts. Be careful with it. *Do not* use it to polish nonferrous metals, lest you polish off the details.

Appendix III–Brushes and Paints

BRUSH SELECTION

Synthetic bristle brushes will work reasonably well in water-based emulsion paints, but paints using thinners such as alcohol or lacquer thinner will degrade some of them.

Bristle brushes of China hog, horsehair, or oxhair are better for oil paint, varnish, and shellac. They will give a more even coat; there will be less spatter; and they resist ordinary solvents.

Paint rollers: Buy the best, with removable cylinders, for ease in cleaning. A roller with dried paint on it is as useless as a brush in the same condition. Rollers are available in a variety of widths and naps, suitable for trim or for covering large surfaces and for handling enamels or latex paints. But give them as much care as you would your brushes.

Shaped synthetic sponges for painting are often handy for tricky corners or cutting straight lines, but they generally are not used for large areas.

DIRTY PAINT BRUSHES

Shame on you for letting it happen! Fortunately, there are commercial brush cleaners on the market that will clean brushes that have dried latex or oil paint on them. They are somewhat expensive, and the fumes are dangerous in an enclosed space. But for dried latex paints they are about the only recourse. There are also less expensive powders to be dissolved in hot water which are available for cleaning dried oil paint brushes. If you wish to make your own solution you can soak the brushes overnight in 4 tablespoons of trisodium phosphate per quart of hot water. Comb out the bristles next day with a steel wire brush, starting at the heel, then rinse in warm water. If this doesn't get it, try soaking again in a fresh hot mixture overnight and repeat the procedure, or else use the more expensive commercial mix. Stiff shellac-coated brushes can be soaked in denatured alcohol; but a hot borax-water or ammonia-water solution is cheaper. Rinse in warm water afterwards.

Do not leave brushes in the paint bucket overnight. They become paint-soaked in the heel; the bristles become bent (often permanently), rendering the brush useless. When finished painting for the day, wash the brush out in whatever solvent is compatible with the paint you have used. Then wash it in warm soap-water and rinse. Next, wrap it in Kraft paper, so it will hold its shape while drying.

Oil paint brushes can be rinsed out cheaply and effectively in mineral spirits, which can be purchased in bulk at paint stores. Unlike turpentine, the mineral spirits allow the paint to settle to the bottom of the rinse pail. Then by careful decanting next morning the bulk of the spirits can be used again.

PAINTING TIPS

Dip brush only about half-way into the paint (or solvent). Cleaning paint out of the heel of the brush is difficult; and if you paint overhead with a full brush or one that still has solvent in the heel, you will find that it runs out of the heel, down your wrist, and down your arm.

A little detergent or aerosol in latex or other water-based paints will make them flow more evenly on slick or pebbly surfaces. Laboratory aerosol, for making water wetter, may be purchased from chemical supply houses such as Fisher.

Paint cans are less apt to spatter on you and the surrounding area if you: 1) punch a hole in the rim of the paint can to let the excess paint drip back into the can; 2) cover the lid with a paint cloth when hammering the top down. Use a mallet rather than a hammer to keep from deforming the lid. Don't pry up the lid with chisels!

Look at the directions on the back of paint cans! There are so many different formulations of paints and thinners that you cannot assume that all paints are alike. Just because a paint is shiny, it is not necessarily thinned with turpentine; in this day and age, water or lacquer thinner may be indicated, and some paints are not to be thinned at all. Failure to heed specific directions is one of the most common causes of paint failures.

REMOVING OLD DRIED PAINT FROM WOOD
OR METAL SURFACES

Needless to say the formulae for stripping paint *do not* apply to fine arts objects such as polychrome sculpture or paintings. That is a specialized field in itself.

Commercial Paint Removers

Let the treated object stand a short while, covered with burlap in order to prevent solvents from evaporating too quickly. Then rub off the old paint with a piece of burlap or coarse cloth while the remover is still damp. Flush with water, *if* it is the kind of remover that calls for this action. Steel wool is sometimes recommended for removing the paint, but it is too dangerous for wood or nonferrous metals. These commercial removers have strong fumes; some pose fire hazards; and some will attack your hands. Be careful!

Home-Brewed Removers

One type of paint remover can be made by combining two parts of turpentine and one part of aqua ammonia. Use plenty of ventilation, as the ammonia is quite strong. The ammonia will discolor some hardwoods, and if left on cuprous objects too long without rinsing will cause formation of cuprous salts. A stronger variant is two parts of denatured alcohol and one part of aqua ammonia. This is particularly effective in removing old lacquer from brass and copper ware. But to be most effective (and to prevent irritation to the eyes and nose), the work should be enclosed in a bell jar or other sealed chamber.

Another homemade remover is a solution of four tablespoons of washing soda or tri-sodium phosphate per quart of hot water mopped on the object. Being aqueous, this solution will swell wood.

Lye Solutions

Warning: Lye solutions are often recommended for removing stubborn paint, but if lye gets in your eyes it will permanently blind you, and it also eats your skin. Lye solutions swell wood, degrade the fibers, and permanently discolor many woods. Are you sure that you want to use it?

These above methods for removing paint film are not to be construed as encouraging one to strip and refinish museum furniture. A knowledge of furniture finishes and their care is a specialized skill. If you want to try this on your personal furniture, that is your business; but it is *not* your function as a curator.

A final warning: rags covered with paint or solvents should be washed in soap and water or discarded in a covered metal can, which should be emptied daily. Paint-soaked rags or steel wool are spontaneously flammable. It is too late to say you are sorry when the fire truck rolls up.

Appendix IV–Selected Chemical Names

1. Aqua ammonia (ammonium hydroxide) usually available from drug stores. The so-called "household ammonia" is a weaker solution, containing soap.
2. Blue vitriol or bluestone (copper sulphate)
3. Borax (sodium tetraborate)
4. "Calgon" (sodium hexametaphosphate)
5. Carbolic acid (phenol)
6. Caustic potash or potash lye (potassium hydroxide)
7. Caustic soda, or soda lye (sodium hydroxide)
8. Chalk (usually calcium carbonate but may also be made of steatite or magnesium carbonate).
9. Copperas, or green vitriol (ferrous sulphate)
10. Denatured alcohol (ethyl alcohol which contains a small percentage of additives, rendering it unfit to drink and therefore free of alcohol tax).
11. Epsom Salts (magnesium sulphate)
12. Glaubers Salts (sodium sulphate)
13. Grain alcohol, or ethyl alcohol (ethanol), usually distilled at 97½%, or 195 proof, and generally made from cereal grains. It is the "grain neutral spirits" in alcoholic drinks, and therefore subject to heavy taxation. Usually the cheaper "denatured" alcohol is therefore used in formulae where potability is not involved.
14. Gypsum (calcium sulphate with bound water); when heated and the water is driven off becomes plaster of Paris.
15. Hypo (sodium *thio*sulphate, not sodium *hypo*sulphite)
16. Litharge (lead oxide)
17. Liver of sulphur (potassium sulphide)
18. Lunar caustic (silver nitrate)
19. Muriatic acid, or marine acid (hydrochloric acid)
20. Oil of vitriol or Vitriol (sulphuric acid)
21. Potash or pearl ash (potassium carbonate)
22. Prussian blue (ferric ferrocyanide)
23. Prussic acid (hydrocyanic acid)
24. Quicklime or burnt lime (calcium oxide)
25. Red lead (lead oxide)
26. Rochelle salt (sodium potassium tartrate)

27. Sal ammoniac (ammonium chloride)
28. Sal-soda or washing soda' (crystalline sodium carbonate)
29. Saltpeter, Chile (sodium nitrate)
30. Saltpeter, Niter (potassium nitrate)
31. Slaked lime (calcium hydroxide) made from quicklime mixed with water.
32. TSP washing powder (tri-sodium phosphate) also called sodium phosphate, tri-basic.
33. Verdigris (copper acetate)
34. Waterglass (sodium silicate)
35. White lead (lead carbonate)
36. White vitriol or white copperas (zinc sulphate)
37. Wood alcohol or methylated alcohol or methylated spirits (methanol) distilled from wood—poisonous if taken internally.

This is only a partial listing, and if there are other names of chemicals whose old or modern equivalents elude you, you will find them in the:
HANDBOOK OF CHEMISTRY AND PHYSICS, A Ready Reference Book of Chemical and Physical Data, Edited by Hodgman, Weast, and Selby. Published by Chemical Rubber Company, 2310 Superior Avenue, N.E., Cleveland, Ohio. Revised annually since 1914.

Whether or not you have scientific training, you will find this handbook invaluable for its thousands of tables of condensed information on mathematics, properties of materials (chemical and thermal), formulae of industrial chemicals and plastics, tables on solubility of various materials, etc. Even if you cannot use or understand more than a small fraction of the material enclosed, it will pay you to have a copy. Since it runs about 3,000 pages, it may take a while to find what you want, or to realize that the information is there; but the more you use it, the more you will become familiar with its diverse range of useful material.

Book design by Gary G. Gore, Vanderbilt University Press